MW01246036

I dedicate this book to Daniel

Kevin Bernard

1996

AUSTIN MACAULEY PUBLISHERS™

LONDON • CAMBRIDGE • NEW YORK • SHARJAH

A CIP catalogue record for this title is available from the British Library.

ISBN 9781788487047 (Paperback)
ISBN 9781788487054 (ePub e-book)

www.austinmacauley.com

First Published 2023
Austin Macauley Publishers Ltd®
1 Canada Square
Canary Wharf
London
E14 5AA

I had never experienced turbulence like that before; I felt myself holding onto my seat as I looked around at the worried faces of my fellow passengers. Just minutes earlier, the captain had announced that due to snow and bad weather, we would be rerouted to Chicago, and now, suddenly and without warning, we were going to land. The intensity and speed with which we hit the runway at Boston's Logan Airport seemed overwhelming; however, my fear was quickly replaced with a feeling of anxiety of the unknown. Hours later after having negotiated my way through the immigration procedures, I found myself navigating through Boston's infamous subway system, the MBTA as it's known to the locals, trying to rationalise my impulsive decisions over the past three days that had brought me across the Atlantic on a whim and a phone call.

I had met Kim a year before while on a shoestring trip around the United States. The trip had lasted three months, and during the penultimate week, I had decided to take a break from my NYC routine, my temporary base, and make a weekend of it in Boston. I had thirty-six hours, a return Amtrak ticket and fifty bucks with which to make it all work. I arrived in Boston early on a Saturday morning and after spending some time meandering around its open spaces and taking in its skyline, I decided to make my way to Cambridge, the home of the famous Harvard University.

I still remember her sitting there in the middle of Harvard Square, dressed in slightly alternative gear, big fly glasses and short mousy brown hair. I sat for a minute, placed my backpack down and took in the environment. All around were artists and exhibitionists punting their talents. People from all walks of life seemed to congregate here. I found myself gazing at her through a group of jugglers, thus not appearing to be staring. The wind was blowing, and I remember this caused her hair to flutter around her soft face; this only increased my intrigue, and I could bear it no more. I walked over, touched her on the shoulder and commented on the dexterity of the jugglers, which had up until that moment had her fixated. An hour later, we were walking hand in hand down the embankment of the Charles River. It was a beautiful afternoon. Boston had, within a short space of five hours, been transformed from a cold stark Amtrak station to a beautiful romantic paradise. Our walking would be interspersed by moments of intense discussions of our immediate environment; each discussion and attempt at gaining further insight into our respective personalities. We were after all perfect strangers from opposite sides of the world.

That evening, to my delight, both because I had nowhere to stay and because I was smitten, she invited me to her home. She lived with her mother, a short corpulent woman who seemed to be carrying an emotional heaviness. She was pleasant enough but understandably wary of the uninvited foreigner her daughter had brought home. I tried to allay her mother's fears through a constructive discussion about myself; she was typically American, but I took a liking to her.

She felt it and reacted with kindness. Kim and I spent the rest of the night in her converted attic bedroom, listening to music, discussing theatre, art and our favourite authors. We spent the next day in each other's arms sitting in one of the many small parks dotted in and around the city. That evening, I reluctantly boarded my Amtrak train bound for New York, and a week later, I was in London.

Three days before my eventful touchdown in Boston, I had been driving around the west coast of Ireland with three friends. We were in our early twenties and out for some fun. I had my first real job starting in two weeks at a multinational, and my world adventure which had started a year before in New York had run its course. It was during the middle of this trip late at night during a house party that I drunkenly walked into a private room and decided against my better judgment to make an international call. I clearly remember fumbling through my little phone book, all the time looking to see if anybody would notice the excitement of making spontaneous contact with friends across the world combined with the fact I was stealing the call all added to the suspense. I came across Kim's number; I looked at the time and decided to give it a try. It rang, her mother picked up and remembered me, almost seemed relieved to hear my voice. After exchanging pleasantries, she promptly passed the phone to Kim. The call lasted all of about five minutes. I said goodbye, hung-up, walked downstairs and went to sleep, everything was about to change. Kim was in trouble.

The next day, I awoke early and took my closest friend aside and explained that I needed to get to Boston ASAP. We packed the car and sped back to Dublin. On arrival, I set about organising funds and buying an air ticket to Boston. I had to borrow most of the money from friends and credit card the rest. I tried to ignore my impending job start. The next day, while in transit in Heathrow, I put another short call through to Kim, explaining that I would be in Boston in seven hours and couldn't wait to see her. She reacted with complete calmness like I was taking the local bus from a neighbouring suburb; I loved her American naivety, I embraced it. I couldn't wait to see her!

Walking up to her house that evening in Southie, which I had to find from memory, I found the door ajar. With trepidation, I knocked, waited and knocked again. "Hello!" she exclaimed. Then she finally appeared. "You cut your hair?" she exclaimed again.

"Hello, Kim," I replied as I embraced her in the little corridor leading into her house. It was obviously much time had passed since we had last seen each other. She seemed different, both physically and in her demeanour. She shut the front door and led me upstairs to her loft.

Grandparents

My story starts about a year ago, 8000 miles away, it was a clear summer evening in January 1996, and I checked my speedometer. It checked back at 130 and hadn't moved much for over 16 hours, except for the obligatory fuel stops. Nothing much to stop for in the desert, to be honest. My road atlas sat snugly on the passenger seat to my left, strategically angled for quick referencing; my cigarettes occupied the same seat. The rest of the car was full of everything you might expect for a move across the country. Some old suitcases piled up in the backseat, a few kitchen accessories, a beige desktop computer box, Tupperware and my parent's old microwave from the late '80s.

It had been an arduous journey, just me and the National Road; my sanity was kept in check by a consistent mix of Roger Waters and my Peter Stuyvesant. It wasn't so much a goodbye but an escape. I much like the country had been free for all of two minutes and albeit I had no idea what was going to happen or even if it would work. I just had to escape. The route itself, a 1,400 km stretch of National Road stretching from Cape Town to Johannesburg, was a well-beaten path for me. Like a salmon, I had been returning to my city of birth since I could remember. My most recent trip took place about a year ago when I had decided with a friend to hitchhike 1,400 for a week to go clubbing.

Growing up in a strict Catholic family in a backwater suburb of Cape Town during the late apartheid years had taken its toll. Since I could remember, I had never felt at home; there had always been this inclination that this is not real, there must be something more authentic. It had always seemed I was living on some sort of stage, where everything was a prop or fake and could be demolished in a second.

Joburg was very close; the landscape was becoming more apocalyptic as the kilometres rolled by. One lane had become two a while back, three lanes were my cue to notch it up a little; 130 was not going to do it anymore. The city, a relentless juggernaut, an energy supernova, demanded you had to meet it head-on or go home. I knew the drill, I pushed the accelerator down hard; the landscape sped up, the highway snaked through the koppies for what seemed like a few seconds and then suddenly as if I had transcended a wormhole the city was just there, dressed in wealth, bound by a labyrinth of freeways and if to serve as some sort of warning illuminated by a constant barrage of lightning.

Some cities are stark and foreboding, some beautiful, unwelcoming and aloof, but this place was different; it was ugly and brash but as long as you had the energy, you were welcome. I thought I had arrived home, little did I know at that stage that it would be but a mere conduit.

I would spend the next two months living with my terminally ill grandfather and his ferocious wife, my grandmother, a bombastic controlling woman whose outdated views of the world seemed totally out of sync with the events in the country. In some sense, I had swapped one prison for another. They lived on a massive erf in one of the city's leafy suburbs. South Africa in 1996 was a country in massive transition, and it was no more evident than in that house. Built 30 priors during the 'glory' days or, depending on where you lived, the 'glory' days, it embodied a lifestyle that no longer seemed attainable in then-contemporary South Africa. Its expansive lands, majestic driveway and large main house complete with outside toilet for the black workers and maids seemed to be struggling to hold onto an era that was fast slipping away. If there was any doubt about the brave new world the country had entered into, the high walls, burglar bars, built-in security and alarms were a stark reminder we were not in the '60s anymore.

Living there was nothing more than complete and utter hell; the expectation was clear, I would pay rent in return for full board, albeit my obligations didn't stop with paying the rent. I was also pressed into service as the garden boy and, as my grandmother was unable to drive, the errand boy. The original idea was that I would live there for a few months until I got on my feet, established myself at my new job and moved into my place. However, it soon became apparent that a third force was at work; behind my back, it was decided rather malevolently that it would best for all concerned that I stay as long as possible to help, especially considering my grandfather's terminal illness. My family were masters at emotional blackmail and psychological exploitation, none of these concepts were even apparent to me those days.

Control was not a foreign concept to me; it had always been there, whether imposed by my strict parents, even stricter Catholic upbringing complete, with private school Catholic education or the state and thus by implication of the threat of military conscription. Control is rather insidious, the obvious part being the rules seem innocuous enough; however, it's the psychological abuse that eats you out like cancer. It's often as it was in my case that you only realise you were a victim many years later. That thing about hindsight.

Still at what felt like the start of an adventure, most of this just seemed business as usual; I was generally filled with a large sense of optimism. Don't get me wrong, I was happy to do my bit and I fully realised just how vulnerable my grandparents were. I just would have preferred to be given the freedom to choose.

My new routine soon took shape fairly quickly, waking up to a cooked tasteless breakfast, which always seemed too much. I drove about 50 km to my office job, where I would pass the day sitting in front of a computer screen completely lost at what I should or shouldn't be doing. I was going outside every chance I could to suck on a cigarette. I had joined as a junior software developer having shown an interest in programming years earlier at school; this eventually led me to do a tertiary education in the field which had ultimately led to me to the position in which I found myself at that point, gainfully employed, surrounded by a bunch of smart people doing smart things. At some level, I felt a sense of accomplishment; I wasn't even 21 and already I was earning more than my father, for which I later heard he had something to say about. In reality, I felt miserable, totally lost directionless, however, full of energy, an explosive combination.

After a soul-destroying day and half a box of cigarettes, I would religiously get back into my car and drive the 50 km back to my grandparents' house. The drive to and from work was the most liberating time of the day, albeit the drive back was better than the drive there, for obvious reasons. The combination of awesome roads, high speed, good music and cigarettes gave me the feeling I was flying. This indeed kept me sane.

The process by which one entered the house was similar to what I would assume entering a high secure embassy post 9/11. Of course, 9/11 was still a few years off, so I had nothing to relate to. The house had an external gate and internal gate, each with two manual chains and locks, requiring the driver to get out, leave the engine running and open the gate, drive-in, stop and close the gate behind, before proceeding to the next. Once and only once the car had made it into the secure area was it safe for my grandmother to open the security gate on the front door, which led to the kitchen, a common design of houses of that era.

Upon entering the house, my overcooked dinner would be waiting. The kitchen itself was nothing to write home about except for the unique feature it had, a security door to the rest of the house. Thinking back, I would have dinner alone locked in a kitchen; moreover, I would think this was normal. After dinner, it was time to help my dying grandfather with a bed bath and other such tasks; some evenings, special tasks would be assigned that would involve painting or garden work. I just got on with it. I hope I helped in some small way. For solitude, I would sit in my car and smoke and listen to the car radio or play tapes; it didn't look that strange, as I was not allowed to smoke in the house, thus the car seemed like a good place to spend my evenings, this whilst my grandmother took in the evening news.

Tuesday evening was student night at the Doors, an alternative club located in the city centre. For the most part, those days the city centre was fast becoming a no-go area for reasons of security and social depravity; however, this only added to the adventure of going out there at night. Every Tuesday was the same. I would shepherd the car out of the compound of a house I lived in, out the side roads of the suburb and onto the M1 and head straight into town; you knew you were getting close when there was a dearth of people and litter seemed to be strewn everywhere. This was one of my favourite things to do. I was up for anything, I would smoke, drink and dance until the club closed. I loved the music, the atmosphere and the crazy people I would meet there, which would inevitably lead to discussions about life and dreams. I met two types of people those days, those that we're happy with their lot, like the Charlize Theron lookalike who worked at bank processing cheques for a living. I wonder what happened to her? Then there were the others that talked about a particular dream, leaving or doing something different, but that is where it ended. Those vanished as soon as the music stopped. I was in this group; driving back to the suburbs, I seemed to put my dreams back into my cubby hole.

On arriving back, I was greeted with the scary prospect of opening two gates in succession manually in the dead of night. It helped to be drunk, as it somehow numbed the apprehension. I did, however, feel exposed and thought it prudent to drive around the street a few times shining my car lights in the act of reconnaissance to increase my chances of not getting high-jacked, a common occurrence those days by the way. Nevertheless, without fail, my grandmother would be waiting for me like Florence Nightingale at the kitchen door with a torch, never happy and questioning the time I had chosen to return with a reference to work in the morning. By this time, I had sobered up somewhat and would politely wish her goodnight.

I remember a particular time when I met an Australian girl, I think the first Australian I had ever met. I met her one of those nights at the doors; we got chatting and besides being mesmerised by her accent, which at the time seemed so exotic, she was also the first person I ever met that ran away to join a circus. I had read about these people in books etc. but never had I met the real McCoy. The combination of her exotic voice and life stories was intoxicating, so much so that I couldn't get enough and agreed to drive her home 100 km to the east of the city. I remember dropping her off at one of these brick railway houses in the East rand. I went in just for a moment and noticed a few strange people hanging about, so I thought it best to leave soonest, which I did. The drive was incredibly long, and I was surprised at just how immense the city was; not surprisingly, I arrived back later than usual, only to find my grandmother had called the police and filed a missing person report. To this day, I am not sure if she was more upset that I might have been apprehended by the tsotsis or that I was late for my promised engagement of mowing the lawn that morning.

This routine continued for almost two months. My grandfather steadily worsened; his cancer, which had started as a skin melanoma, had spread everywhere. Every morning after breakfast, before setting off to work, I would spend a few minutes with him. I found it a surreal experience. He couldn't say much or do anything, except lie there writhing in pain, totally trapped in his body, in his room, in his house behind the walls in a suburb under siege from its past.

Then one day, everything stopped for me. An emergency staff meeting at the office was convened; the boss, in tears barely holding it together, somehow managed to blurt out that the company was on life support and as such layoffs were imminent. I drove home that day unemployed; my new life, over before it had even begun.

Daniel

I hadn't been unemployed for too long before a friend of mine, whom I had casually got to know through my cousin, had suggested a particular recruitment agent that I might consider faxing my CV too, to secure a new job. Without giving it too much thought, I decided to take her up on her recommendation.

The agent in question was a British woman, in her late 40s; again, I found her accent intoxicating. I seemed to add credibility to foreign accents those days and was sure she would be able to help me secure another job. She worked from a converted pool house on her property in one of the many golf estates dotted around Johannesburg's northern suburbs. Golf estate was just another name for the gated community with a built-in golf course. Middle-class luxury living for the time was designed to keep the world out and the residents blissfully ignorant, almost a metaphor for the country, which up and till recently had kept itself very isolated from the rest of the world. If you were middle class and living in Johannesburg those days, your feet seldom touched the natural earth. You seemed to always be between a mall, office and fake-gated community separated by varying lengths of car journeys.

After a brief Q/A session, she exclaimed that it wouldn't be a problem for someone with my skills to secure a job at a local financial company; my skills were great and that sector was always looking for fresh blood, and she would be able to secure an interview in no time. Then she did something strange, she put down my CV, looked at me straight and with this brash UK northern attitude, asked me, "Kevin, you don't want to work, do you? You want to travel, right?" It was like some invisible chain had been broken; somebody had finally acknowledged there was another way; ironically, it was a recruitment agent no-less, someone charged with keeping the economy supplied with fresh zombies.

"YES," I exclaimed with a smile.

"Right, you need to meet my son, Daniel," she replied at which point she frog-marched me into the main house and asked me to wait in the kitchen whilst she tried to wake her son up. After a few minutes, a freshly woken, deshelled-looking Daniel appeared brandishing a freshly lit cigarette out the corner of his mouth.

"Howzit, Kevin right?" he muttered. My life would never be the same again.

I didn't expect a job interview that day, but that's exactly what I got. Each of us sizing the other up for mission suitability. By the time I had walked into that house, I had already made up my mind to take the risk and expunge my old life. I was just looking for a partner with the right mix of guts, madness and cash to go with. Although he was two years younger than me, it turned out he had more travel experience, having backpacked through the UK, Europe and Israel. At that stage, I had only done Ireland and London. To be honest, Ireland didn't count as I stayed with family. We spent about an hour in the kitchen that morning, each explaining our respective experience, laying out our cashflow situation and reasons for wanting to do it at all. It soon became apparent that Daniel was like nobody else I had met before; he was introverted but brash, very slightly built but confident in his ability, but what impressed me most was that he seemed to have a Ph.D. in survivability. However, I suspected he was ruthless and lacked my level of empathy. He was perfect. I needed somebody that would keep it together under stress and maybe teach me the ropes. What I lacked in experience and ruthlessness, I made up for in cash and enthusiasm. That morning we hired each other.

Near the end of our discussion, the topic of where and when came up; several suggestions were made on his part, all seemed very hard indeed. However, we both agreed with my idea: Fly to NYC, buy a custom van, fill it with beer and women and drive the country flat. America had always been on my radar not so much as an endpoint, but as a place I would want to experience at least once in my life. Also coming from South Africa, it seemed the country most similar, both being large swaths of land with a settler mentality and English speaking. I wasn't looking for any culture or an exoteric experience at that stage; I just wanted an adventure and what better country for a road trip than the USA.

Upon leaving, I thanked his mum and explained that I would in the coming days pack my stuff and drive home, sell my car, cash-out my savings account and say goodbye to my parents. I wanted to be back in two weeks, as we had targeted to get to NYC in April; it was now beginning March 1996. I had long since felt so determined and motivated. I finally felt I was going in the right trajectory.

The ensuing days went exactly as planned. I drove the 1400 km home, sold my car to a used car dealer and cashed-out my savings. Being back at home after leaving only two months before being fired upped the ante with regards to the atmosphere at home. My parents were notably disappointed on the one hand but generally excited on the other; the latter being more true of my mum's attitude. I was sure my dad had somewhat written me off at this stage. I didn't care. I had no time for a fearful scarcity attitude towards life; hell, I was going to America; they don't do scarcity very well. My poor mother who at that stage had only been to Ireland seemed to secretly wish she could go with me. The adage of fools venturing where angels fear to tread was bandied about a few times; this only emboldened me more than ever. My girlfriend of three years was also told; that went well, not. Two weeks passed quickly and soon after a rather long greyhound bus journey, I was back in Johannesburg; this time, I chose to crash with an acquaintance. The days of staying with my family were over; this was a new chapter. I would never see my grandfather again, as he died soon after.

In the next three weeks, we set about trying to organise ourselves. Daniel, for his part, was working at a local high-end restaurant trying to get his cash flow in order, whilst I spent my days brainstorming on the plan. It was a crazy time; we spent a lot of time together going out and partying. Those days, Rocky Street was still a reasonably safe albeit edgy nightspot. Oftentimes we would while away our time there, oftentimes in one of the bars discussing our upcoming trip. I wouldn't say we ever became friends, but we started to develop mutual respect for each other's devoutness to the idea: that there was something better than the status quo.

Daniel was an adrenaline junkie of the classic sort; he owned a motorcycle, and he drove the thing to a near-death speed, often with me on the back, sometimes high on cocaine. It soon became apparent we would compete rather than complement each other. We competed for attention, for women, for status, for everything. However, it was too late. This was my travel partner for better or worse. It was our mutual respect that seemed to keep the peace so to speak.

In between the chaos of the cocaine-filled nights racing on the highways with his motorcycle friends, who all seemed to hold us in the highest esteem for actually having the guts to even think about going, we accomplished what needed to be done to go. Airline tickets, forex and the piste de resistance, a great big American road atlas was purchased. The atlas enthralled us, and mapping out our proposed routes became our famed pastime those days before leaving. On paper, the size of the country was impressive. This huge dollop of land crisscrossed by an almost unending system of roads, all seemingly meticulously laid out.

One of our biggest challenges was getting an initial place to stay in NYC, as none of us knew anyone. We knew it would take some time to purchase a custom van suitable to our needs and that we could use for accommodation, and in those early weeks, we wanted to keep costs as low as possible because for sure, we knew the burn rate in NYC would be high at the best of times. However, luckily this resolved itself in the most divine of ways. One night whilst out clubbing, we ran into a recent friend of Daniel, Brian, and we got to chatting about our plans and challenges. Now unbeknown to us, it turned out that Brian was a bastard child to an American serviceman that was stationed in the UK during the late '70s. Brian had moved with his mother to South Africa sometime later for one or another reason.

Brian was a resourceful kinda guy, and it wasn't long before he hatched a plan for us. The idea centred around him coming around the next evening to Daniel's house to put a long-distance call through to his dad, an expensive proposition those days from South Africa to say the least. I got the impression he never spoke much to his dad; maybe he saw this as a way he could connect with him without the high cost. The call started and the conversation went well. Brian seemed to have a great rapport with his father; this was evident in the conversation flow that ensued. After about 30 minutes into the call, he laid the bait and explained that two of his best friends were coming to NYC city for an epic road trip. The plan worked; we not only had a place to stay for a couple of days, but we were going to be picked up from the airport. Euphoric, we set about getting to know all the details we needed to come across as Brian's supposed best friends; we had two weeks to do the debrief, and we wanted to come across as authentic as possible.

Not long after, we managed to bundle ourselves on the cheapest flight we could find to NYC, A Balkan airline service with multiple stopovers and change in Sofia. It took almost 16 hours to get to Bulgaria after stopping over in Kenya. Disembarking at the airport in Sofia was a poignant moment for me; for the first time since we hatched the plan, I felt some angst that I had potentially bitten off more than I could chew. This feeling was exacerbated by the stark contrast between Johannesburg's leafy northern suburbs littered with golf estates and glistening pools juxtaposed to what I saw flying in: an ugly concrete monster frozen down in a sheet of ice. What an ugly place; I was glad to leave. Our second flight stopped over rather unexpectedly on the picturesque island of Malta; it seemed charming, but little did I know I would move there 20 years later and write this story from that island. Those days, you could smoke on the flights, provided of course you sat in the smoking section; this we relished. However, if I had known how expensive a box of cigarettes would be in NYC, I might have been a bit more sparing.

Landing in NYC a few hours later seemed less than thrilling to be honest; the plane seemed to descend in a cloud that reached from the heavens to the tarmac. We saw nothing of the famed skyline; the only thing I remember that stood out was that everybody started clapping as soon as we touched down. This I had never experienced in South Africa in all my flights; still to this day, I am not sure what they were clapping about, the fact we made it all?

A little while later, we were confronted with a large burly bearded man in his 40s wearing blue dungarees and brandishing a sign with our names. Standing next to him was a teenage boy, his son. "Hi, I'm Dan Weber, Brian's dad, welcome to NYC," he exclaimed. We had made it; well, we had made it to the start, at least we had started it, started something, anything. I felt a small sense of achievement. Our drive from JFK to Palisade Park, New Jersey, where we would camp out for the next two weeks wasn't without incident. At some point, Dan managed to get us pulled over by the police for not adhering to a 'no right turn' sign, something I had never seen in my life before. It was almost entertaining to see this whole thing unfold in front of me, as I had seen it many times on television before. However, I did feel bad for the guy; it wasn't a small sum and he had gone out of his way to pick us up.

The Webers

Pulling up to the house in one of those nondescript New Jersey neighbourhoods seemed innocuous in itself; however, for me, it was my coming to America moment. Everything seemed novel to me: the side of the road we drove on, the cute post boxes and the ubiquitous basketball hoops lining the streets; nothing was arbitrary in my mind. To me, it felt I was in a different place, a different world and that felt great.

The Weber residence was to be our temporary home for at least a week or so whilst we got on our feet. Dan was a larger-than-life character, straight-talking and sporting long hair much like us; we felt very much at home around him. Surprisingly, he worked as a full-time cleaner, not something I had ever seen before; White people didn't do cleaning jobs back home. I was bemused at how he was able to support a family on a cleaner's salary. His wife was a bit off, Armenian by descent. I never felt that comfortable with her. I suspected they had marital issues, but I kept it at arm's length. Their two children – a boy and a girl – whose names I forget, seemed to be cookie cuts outs of kids their age in the area. They were far less naïve then kids their age back home, but their world was very small, dumbed down to local and or national trends, media and consumerism habits. Both accepting and friendly enough but somehow strange at the same time. Dan was the only one who had travelled and thus the only one we could connect to. We were so thankful to his son back in Johannesburg and tried to answer all the questions that were put to us, sugar-coating where necessary; we thought that was fine.

Squatting in the Webers' lounge we knew was not sustainable for that long; thus, we hoofed it to get organised. We couldn't rely on their hospitality for too long; to be fair, we were a novelty to them too, but it wasn't going to last. We needed our van and fast. Now Daniel had no driving license, only a South African learner's, which was enough to ride a motorcycle back home, a small detail I ignored when we met. Armed with our atlas, we hired a car on my credit card from a hire joint situated in the middle of Manhattan; what possessed us I don't know, but as I pulled out of that lot driving for the first time on the other side of the road in peak NYC traffic, I felt like a had never driven in my life. It was a struggle to keep on the correct side of the road, and the cacophony of rules confused me; the complexity of driving in NYC could not be overstated coming from South Africa. It was a learning experience and I had to learn quickly. We spent days driving up and down the car lots in New Jersey but could find nothing that suited our budget. Every day, we would try a different area; it took time and we always left disappointed. This dragged on for days, and it eventually started to take its toll.

Living with the Webers during those initial two weeks gave us an incredible insight into the drudgery of New Jersey life. Saturdays were spent at the local mall and evenings were spent shooting hops and hanging out on the streets with friends and neighbours. The discussions ranged from local politics to Vietnam war experiences. This was a blue-collar neighbourhood on the cusp of one of the greatest cities in the world; somehow, Manhattan seemed a world away. Food was a nightmare; nobody cooked. Everything was fast food or failing that served up on two slices of bread. The quintessential peanut butter and jelly sandwich, which soon became a favourite of mine, was the staple comfort food. I was grateful for the experience but equally grateful I hadn't been born there.

We eventually found a van on a trip to Pennsylvania. A bunch of cowboys running a local car-lot saw us coming a mile away and offloaded a beautiful 1984 custom Chevy van for about 2,500 USD. Little did we know at that stage they had sold us a dud. That night, Daniel drove the hire car back whilst I followed him in the van; notwithstanding his lack of licence, we made it back and were now ready to start our trip or so we thought.

The problem with being overly optimistic is that you don't foresee a lot of the details that inadvertently come with grandiose plans. Having bought the van, we now had to face the almost herculean task of getting it insured. For this, we needed it registered with the DMV to get plates, which meant I needed a social security number and an address. This meant spending more time troubleshooting in and around New Jersey and dealing with bureaucratic tediousness when all we wanted to do was drive. Luckily, the system provided us with a loophole at least that is how we saw it; those days, temporary plates were provided on all vehicle sales valid for four weeks, a grace period if you will. We saw this as an opportunity to park the registration process for a while and get out, and that's what we did. Looking back, it was a huge risk to say the least.

So after two days, we packed the van and drove north. To be honest, we had no real plan of where we wanted to go, just an incredible sense of adventure that kept pushing us forward. The more we drove, the more we wanted to drive; we almost hated stopping. After about a week, we had driven up the I95 to Canada, crossed the border and re-entered the USA. The time had been a trial run of sorts to see how Daniel and I coped in the closed space of the van. Routine had set in quickly: every evening before going to sleep, we would need to find a secure place to hold up for the night, cover the windows with blankets and towels for privacy, taking turns to sleep on the one bed the van offered. It had been cold; we had naively driven north and followed the winter so-to-speak. We would catch the odd shower at truck stops and eat at fast food joints daily, literally punishing our bodies; gone were the days of gourmet Woolworths food we had taken so for granted in our privileged South African life.

On re-entering the US, we found ourselves driving around the streets of Chicago looking for parking. Space was at a premium in US cities and parking was hard to come by and expensive to boot. This was a frustrating lesson we had to learn early on. At some point, I took a wrong turn and entered a one way and suddenly found myself facing off with a taxi approaching in the opposite direction; we both swerved but it was too late. I ended up clipping him and scratching his door. For whatever reason, instead of stopping, I floored the van in some vain attempt to escape. We had no insurance and this had always been on my mind. Like a movie, the taxi turned and bolted after us; our slow cumbersome van was no match for a car, especially in those short one ways we had found ourselves in. Eventually accepting our fate, we stopped. The driver, a Black guy, was understandably angry; however, he seemed to try and exploit the situation. His ramshackle car was full of knocks and dents, and he was adamant we had caused most of them. His animated ranting and raving were soon stopped when Daniel wrestled the van door open with a thud, pointed to our backpacks and exclaimed, "This is all we own; take what you want." Shocked and confused by Daniel's foreign accent and directness, he just stood there dazed.

I just looked on at the events unfolding in front of me. Daniel's street wisdom, garnered in his previous travels and experiences with procuring drugs in Johannesburg's more precarious suburbs, was coming through. It was a great lesson. After a few seconds of which felt like an eternity, Daniel coolly reached for his wallet and pulled out a ten-rand note, about 2 USD, gave it to the guy and managed to convince him it was worth 100 USD. He accepted, and thus using his greed against him, we were able to secure a five-minute window in which to escape the situation. We jumped in the van and fled; we left Chicago without seeing anything and didn't stop until we reached Miami. I felt terrible and my confidence was notably in tatters. I had caused the situation, and Daniel had rescued us; it was a low point for me.

Finding a place to hold up for the nights became another unexpected challenge we had to learn to deal with. Mostly we would use the 24-hour supermarkets and gas station parking facilities. We found the 24-hour presence added both a margin of safety and convenience. However, on a few occasions on our trip down to Miami, we found ourselves, as unwilling spectators, onto drunken fights that would start in and around the van for some reason. On one once such occasion, we decided to park the van in a residential area for the night. Then just as we had readied the van for the evening, we suddenly noticed we were surrounded by an array of blue flashing blue lights. Understandably, some of the residents had become anxious and paranoid and called the cops on us. After a quick explanation, we found ourselves back at a 24-hour supermarket.

We didn't spend long in Miami; just long enough to explore South Beach and witness a couple of gangbangers try to knife each other in the car lot we chose to spend the night in. Soon we were driving through the Florida Keys on our way to Key West; still to this day one of the most spectacular drives I have taken to date. We wanted to spend some time in Key West and enjoy what it had to offer, a well-deserved break after driving aimlessly for the past two weeks. At this stage, we had two challenges approaching like slow-moving train wrecks: first, our temporary plates were expiring in two weeks, after which we wouldn't just be bending the rules, we would be breaking them and secondly, our cash burn rate was very high. Full disclosure at this stage, it was obvious our budgeting had been far too optimistic; this was made worse by the fact that rather contentiously, Daniel had not been able to raise the necessary cash agreed before the trip and with most of the cash invested in the van, we were looking at a pretty dire situation come a few weeks.

Nonetheless, we motored on, choosing to turn a blind eye to the nascent challenges that were around the corner. We enjoyed our time in Key West; it was rather different than anything else I had seen to date. It had a very relaxed almost Caribbean feel to it. We spent a few days there just chilling during the day and drinking at night. We were happy to give the driving a break for the time being and decided instead to turn the van into a makeshift bar. This we achieved by buying a keg of beer and storing it on the back seat. We met a lot of people this way, mostly Australians and Kiwis that had rolled into port on one of the many boats as crew. Inevitably, our van became synonymous with sin, as it became almost notorious for its beer on tap. People would come and just hang out, drink, play music, smoke pot and party. It was also a great opportunity to learn from some of the most seasoned travellers we had met. These Antipodeans were a different breed altogether when compared with the typical European types we had met before; they seemed fearless and had this ability to 'wing-it' a skill that I picked up and have used successfully ever since.

On our penultimate day in Key West, we found ourselves rather uncharacteristically in a cocktail bar. A busy place, so much so that we had to share a large table with a bunch of strangers. Before long, we were chatting to a group of three girls from Syracuse, Upstate New York. This was a pivotal moment in our trip, although we didn't know it yet; meeting them would change everything and give us the leverage we didn't know we needed. They were three smart university graduates, all but one of them had recently moved to NYC to start their careers; the other had just accepted a government job in the Pentagon and was waiting to move to Washington, Neleen. She was the most beautiful of the three: she was thin, had a beautiful toothy smile, curly back hair and was sun kissed. The other two: Jenny was a corpulent girl who had just accepted a job in a big NYC advertising bureau, and the last girl was strange, thin, pretty and I think of Mediterranean descent, but aloof and quiet. They were very intrigued by us, our accents, our outlook and our stories, as we were with them.

They had flown down to Florida for two weeks, hired a house in Tampa, to use as their base, rented a black Pontiac firebird, beautiful machine, and decided to visit the Keys for the weekend. Rather serendipitously, they ran into us, and all our lives changed. After a night of drinking at the bar, Neleen and Daniel had become infatuated with each other. I will admit I was very jealous; however, I had my marijuana and my beer to cope. Later that night, we all hopped in the van and drove to their motel. Daniel hand in hand with Neleen and the two girls went inside to sleep on the three beds that were there, whilst I agreed to stay in the van. Later that night, just as I was dozing off in my drunken state, I heard a knock on the window with this voice, "Kevin, Kevin, we need to use the van." Clearly, they were not going to get the privacy they needed in the motel room and thus decided to requisition the van. I was a little shocked and didn't answer at first, then slowly, I rolled out, glancing a smile at them both and stumbled into somebody's bed inside. I have no recollection of the rest of the night. The next morning after we woke, we spent the morning chilling by the motel pool and hatched a plan to join them in their house in Tampa for a few days. They gave us their address, and it was decided we would rendezvous there in two days. Admittedly, I saw the opportunity of a place to stay in NYC in the coming future and used this to negotiate away my jealousy with the two love birds. We were going to need a place to stay in NYC, and we were going to need it for free. Our cash flow was becoming a concern; also, the relationship between myself and Daniel had started to show its first cracks. I mean we had only met each other two months before. Bound together with our joint investment in the van, we were dependent on each for survival whilst competing for everything. We were miles from home and alone.

As planned, two days later, we rolled up to the house the girls had hired for their vacation, a large bungalow within walking distance to the beach, perfect place to hang out for a few days. The next few days, we lived with them, mornings were spent blading on the beachfront and afternoons were spent hanging out exploring each other's respective backgrounds and unique life experiences. In the evenings, we cooked together and held pseudo dinner parties. I found Neleen to be the smartest, and I gravitated to her; at this stage, her infatuation with Daniel was starting to wane. I found the whole experience very insightful insofar as getting to know three people of similar age who had grown up in a very different country across the world but had similarly moved away from the safety of home to the great unknown, the big city.

After a few days, it was time for the girls to catch their flight back to NYC; however, the night before, we decided to go clubbing in Tampa. This was the first time since our arrival we had done such a thing, albeit the dream was to be out every night in this great country exploring every party scene we could; the reality was somewhat different. This trip was hard work and expensive, and this kept a lid on some of the more salubrious activities we would have liked to partake in. Two things happened that night: firstly, we hatched the plan that we would drive the van back to NYC and stay with Jenny for a week or so in her flat in Queens, this to help us with the paperwork for our van, which had become this monkey on our back. I had been laying the bait for that all week and for that fact alone, I was happy with the situation with Daniel and Neleen, and secondly, I met a transexual first time in my life, and to be honest, I thought she was beautiful.

The next day, we said goodbye to the girls with a promise to see them again in NYC in a few days. We had been gone for four weeks now; already, we were different people. From then on out, I knew I was never going back to South Africa. Now it was time to go do adult things in NYC before starting the real trip.

NYC

Before long, we found ourselves on the I-95 making our way back to NYC. It was a long drive, and not unlike our drive down to Florida, we were mainly just stopping for fuel. We would take it in turns, two hours' shifts each. Besides the license and the cash flow problem, we were also conscious of a third problem: the van was on its last legs. On our way to Florida on our escape from Chicago, we had decided to stop off in Athens Georgia; we were intrigued by a place in the deep south that could have given rise to a band so progressive as REM. For the previous 8,000 miles, we had had this sneaky suspicion there was something mechanical questionable with the van. It always seemed to struggle at 55 miles and the engine often stalled when idle. It also seemed to take lots of cajoling in the morning to get it running.

Upon entering Athens, we pulled into the first franchised mechanical joint we saw. After explaining to the technician guy, who was about our age and dressed in uniform with his name on it, that we had recently bought the van and had driven about 8000 miles, and we now thought it prudent to get a service and check-up so to speak, he took the keys and told us to wait in the reception area until we were called.

After waiting about half an hour or so, he reappeared, clipboard in hand, brandishing an expression not unlike what you would expect from a surgeon who had just done intricate surgery on a terminal case. He beckoned nervously for us to follow him into the back.

On entering the back of the shop, we saw our van jacked up, hood open and surrounded by three other uniformed technicians, all looking perplexed. On seeing us, one of them interjected, "How many miles have you guys driven this thing? 8,000 miles, that's amazing!" Our hearts sank. We knew then what we had suspected all along; we had been sold a dud. These used car salesmen in Pennsylvania had seen us coming before we even left South Africa. After a humiliating 30 minutes, which was spent explaining to us just how many plug points were shot and how many bits of spark plug were most likely embedded in the engine, we all agreed that they had done what they could and that we should join them for a drink at their local after work. Twenty minutes later, they all piled into the van, and we drove to a pool hall in town. These guys were a lot of fun, and we couldn't think of a better way to drown our sorrows. I don't remember anything of that night, just waking up in the van in my underwear in full view of a school bus full of kids driving past. We had been too drunk to cover the windows with towels that night, whatever.

The trip back to NYC was arduous; from Florida, it's about a 1,600-km haul. The constant driving had started to take its toll on the van; during the day it would overheat. It became almost ritualistic. The van would splutter and konk out; we would then shepherd it to the emergency lane, open the bonnet and simply wait for it to cool down. Without fail every time, the highway patrol would appear and question us on the situation. Although we had foreign accents and looked like hippies, we never experienced problems; just to be safe, the first thing we did was stash our drugs about 100 metres away in the bush. The procedure was always the same: we would be in the van reading or listening to music secretly praying the van would eventually start, then without fail, a patrol car would pull up in front. The officer would get out, put on his hat, wrestle with his gun belt a little and walk up to the van. Always the same discussion, then they would leave explaining we had 24 hours before we would be towed.

Like clockwork, the van would start again after about a two-hour break, and we would once again be on our way. There was no adventure or romanticism in these long drives. I cannot overstate the boredom we experienced on that interstate. It became an endurance test of sorts. It was during these times that certain hard discussions were had between myself and Daniel; for instance, like the one where we agreed that if we were involved in an accident before we had secured insurance and one of us was injured, it was okay for the other to walk away to escape prosecution.

We would eat at these all-you-can-eat joints, basically, huge buffets of cheap food fried up in trans fats. We became experts on exploiting the system by reusing cups for free drinks and hiding food in our belt bags for later consumption. At this stage, we had about four weeks of cash left at the current burn rate.

We arrived in NYC late one evening; the two majestic World Trade centres cut the sky like a modern-day obelisk. The sight gave me goosebumps; the whole scene oozed energy and all around us the frenetic energy was building as we got closer. It reminded me of another long drive I had taken only two months before when I moved to Johannesburg. It kinda felt like home now.

It took us a while to find Jenny's flat. We had already called ahead and left a message on her answering machine for her to expect us that night. She had rented a one-bed basement in a questionable area in Queens. She was both surprised and happy to see us. Her flat was small, dark and cold, but it was a paradise for us; we were so grateful for a place to stay and be out of the van.

Getting the van registered was now the order of the day and that involved the DMV. Our first experience with the DMV in Hoboken left a lasting impression; the decor seemed reminiscent of something out of Eastern Europe, unfit for purpose. The conversation we had with the DMV representative that helped us that day might well have taken place on planet Zog, for it was as intelligible. The guy in question, a young guy, had recently had his tongue pierced, and for love or money, he could not string a sentence together. It was like facing a barrage of spit and broken Slovak after a hard night's drinking. We knew to get anything done in the US you always enlisted the help of an American, and to that, we had the presence of mind to request the help of Dan Weber, who had become our oracle on such things. Dan was as relaxed as they came, but his comment of getting his monkey wrench and ripping that guy's tongue piercing out of his mouth after a long frustrating conversation resonated with me. It was clear that before we could register the van, we would need social security numbers.

A few days later, we found ourselves in the department of social security in NYC to apply for a social security number. I just couldn't believe that we would have to become near citizens to register a vehicle. I thought people would go through a whole immigration procedure or, heaven forbid, get married to get one of these numbers. I had visions of having to do an English test and sing the Star-Spangled Banner before being granted such a number. We looked so out of place in that government bureau; everybody around us was clearly down on their luck and seemed to belong to some ethnic minority group that had recently escaped a war zone somewhere in the world. I doubt any of these people would have swapped the leafy northern suburb Johannesburg lifestyle for Queens as we had. We patiently waited our turn, joking about the situation we found ourselves in; eventually, we were called into an office, and after presenting a few documents and answering yes to every question we were asked, we were issued a number. We only needed one number, as the van would be registered in my name. The following days were spent following up with the DMV and getting quotes for insurance. As money was tight, we were only going to buy the first month's insurance just to get the insurance sticker for our windshield so on face value, the van would look bonafide; however, if after a month we were stopped, we would be in trouble. It was a risk we were stupidly willing to take.

We enjoyed our stay in NYC. We fell into a routine and made the city ours. Even morning we walked to the local bagel shop and gouged on one of the hundreds of options available. Daniel and I wisely took this opportunity to spend some time apart. I would take the subway to Manhattan and spend hours discovering alternative music and book shops and almost ritually end up in Washington Square Park, where I would while away my time reading, people watching or speaking to whatever cute girl I could intrigue with my accent; there were many. Some evenings, we would join the girls in their routine, either being invited to corporate parties with their colleagues or quietly taking in a movie at one of those just off syndicate movie houses, which I had never heard of before. I found the city truly inspiring and full of energy but not just the energy to amass wealth built on a scarcity mindset, which I had been so accustomed to back home, but the energy that involved the creation of something authentic and new no matter what the risk. On the evenings that time permitted, Daniel and I would drive the van down to the Hudson and drink beers out of brown paper bags whilst watching the NY skyline transform from its work attire into its evening dress. With the skyline glittering in the background, we would use the time to discuss what was to become of us; we would question the sanity of what we were doing and, most importantly, try to understand the core reason for driving us to do this. In trying to understand, we would reminisce of the people we had left back home in their routines, in their leafy suburbs, in their country that had been free only for all of two minutes. We never managed to get clarity but always drove back with a hardened resolve to carry on.

Living with Jenny and attending regular meets with her social circle gave us an incredible insight into the corporate workings of the city. Most, if not all, had moved from Syracuse after graduating to start their respective careers in the city. Netscape and just IPO'D a year earlier and the city was a buzz with the talk of the internet and startups.

After what seemed like weeks, but, in reality, had been less than a few days, we were ready to hit the road again. Even at this stage, we didn't have a plan as to what we wanted to achieve; however, we were happy with that. We kept reminding ourselves it was a journey that we were here for. However, since we had arrived in the country, everybody had been talking about this thing called 'Spring Break'; still, to this day, I don't fully understand it. However, it was purported to be the event of the year; it involved consuming copious amounts of alcohol and going home with strangers; we were strongly urged to participate. So the day after we affixed our new plates to our van, we packed up and set off down the I-95 again, destination: Panama City, Florida.

Broke

Driving 1600 km down to Florida, a place we had just come back from a little under a week ago, just for a party did seem a little counterintuitive and, by implication, decadent. There was a whole country out west we desperately wanted to see; however, considering the dire state of our finances, which by now had become a major worry, it was difficult to see how we could continue in any direction west or otherwise. Still, somehow, our intuition was taking us back down to Florida, and we were okay with that. Akin to our trip to NYC, we only stopped for fuel and food, albeit we were becoming far more discerning with prices that we chose to pay for these. Looking for bargains on fuel and only eating at the all-you-can-eat places became the norm. Those days, it was around 1 USD for a gallon of fuel, our van was about as fuel-efficient as a tank; thus, if we could save a cent on a gallon, to us, it was worth it. We also tried to time our van's characteristic breakdowns with lunch breaks. This meant spending about two hours eating small amounts at multiple intervals like some sort of eating marathon. We would camp out at the all-you-could-eat buffets, secretly stashing the odd choice morsel in our belt bags for later consumption. We tried to only eat once a day now. To be honest, this was the first time in my life I thought about food with a scarcity mindset; never in my life before had I needed to worry about where my next meal would come from. We also found ourselves in a self-imposed food desert, obviously having no opportunity to cook and thus buy fresh produce, we were at the mercy of the toxicity served up at these fast-food joints. Living with Jenny the week before had been a reprieve of some sorts with the food situation, and we did take the opportunity to cook both for substance and as a gratuitous act to her, having dinner ready on the odd occasion on her return from work went a long way to keeping us on her good side. After all, we barely knew her and the romance which had bound the two groups of friends had taken on a long-distance nature. Neleen had not been in NYC during our week there as she had gone back to Syracuse.

On arrival in Panama City, we decided to treat ourselves to a night in a motel. After finding a suitable place, of which there was no shortage of options, we set about figuring out how to exploit this spring break weekend. The motel had one small bed and thus like everything scarce on the trip, we had to compete for it, so we decided to flip a coin. At this point in the trip, we had done this a few times already, and I had always lost. None of the outcomes had been life-changing, however, whether it was driving the night shift or getting the tip I had also seemed to lose, this was no exception; that night I slept in the van.

Before bed that evening, we drove to the beach for a walk to stretch our legs. After a while, we happened upon some kids who, by their actions we could see, were high; they must have been about 14 or so. We approached them directly and asked if they had anything spare. After initially denying the situation, they eventually capitulated and agreed to sell us some 'Mississippi wet' as they called it. Happy with our purchase, we drove back to the motel, parked up and rolled two big joints to help us sleep. All I remember was waking up, what seemed hours later, but in reality was only a few minutes, with bright lights and the sounds of hooting all around us. Seemingly, we had forgotten to pull the handbrake and the van had rolled back into the middle of the street, blocking all traffic. On either side, there was a traffic jam a few cars deep. I quickly leapt to the driver seat, turned the key and shot the van back up the driveway. I turned to look at Daniel, high as a kite on the backseat, and we just burst out laughing; how we didn't attract the police that evening I have no idea.

As we walked in and out the many hotels dotted up the down the Pensacola coast over the next few days, we experienced first-hand what this college festival was all about. To say it was a let-down would be understating the hype exponentially. I am not sure what we were expecting, but what we experienced ranged from comical to shocking. Every hotel without fail was a carbon copy of the other. They were filled with gym rats, shirts off or sporting bikinis dancing to the most soulless music I had ever heard. It seemed that each character was on display or for sale somehow. It reminded me of a certain BBC animal kingdom episode. I could almost hear Richard Attenborough's voice in the background, "The alpha gym rat has finally got the attention of the less spotted bikini female and is enticing her with his rendition of the hula R&B style." It was the most inauthentic experience. The closest I had come to this before in my life was a Sokkie I once attended in the West Rand. I had no idea the youth of the world's preeminent country would be so dumbed down. This charade didn't stop at the hotel pool area; it overflowed onto the streets. The town was chokka with convertible vehicles and pickup trucks filled to the brim of the same characters we found at the pool. Almost in convoy, they would drive slowly up and down the main drag as if on some sort of May Day parade in Kyiv. The biggest take away from this was the material wealth these kids had access to; it was unprecedented and unlike anything I had ever seen. Quite in contrast to our wealth situation, which by now was becoming impossible to ignore.

We left Panama City earlier than expected, it wasn't for us, and we had to figure out a solution to our cash flow problem fast. Before having left South Africa, I, fortunately, had the presence of mind to find and contact a few people who had recently completed a road trip across the USA. I did this first to get inspiration and secondly to acquire knowledge and potential contacts. One such contact I had I thought might be able to help with the money situation, a company based in Fort Lauderdale. It was set up years ago by a motley crew of South African surfers from Durban who had moved to the USA and now ran a thatching company. After discussing it with Daniel, we decided to pay them a visit; already being in the state, we thought we had nothing to lose. At this stage, we were eating one meal a day between us. We would share a Big Mac combo meal, to the point of counting the fries; that's how bad things were. Like adversaries, we would watch each other with hawk eyes, as not to be outdone a single calorie. To make matters worse, I had already started to use my emergency credit card; thus, by implication I was going into debt in a foreign currency. It must be said that at this stage, the international capital markets had started to fall out of love with South

Africa, and this was no more evident than the exchange rates that were now available to me on our credit card pre-auths. The foreign exchange volatility I was experiencing had a major impact on my decision never to earn money in a developing country; this lesson served me well in years to come. I saw the depreciating rand as another attack on my freedom, and I was right. The currency never recovered and like the country, it continued to fall to new depths every year.

On arrival in Fort Lauderdale, we phoned ahead and explained briefly our situation; luckily, they were only too happy to see us. That afternoon, we drove to their office on the outskirts of town in some nondescript industrial park. As we walked in, we were greeted by the secretary, also from Durban, judging by her accent, not long after the two owners crowded around us and greeted us. They were happy to see fellow South Africans, as were we, and after a few minutes of reminiscing about the country and explaining our trip, we got down to the business at hand: asking them for work. We were sure they would be able to give us some menial labour. We would have been happy with minimum wage for a few weeks just to tide us over. Rather shockingly, they responded that they only hired illegal Mexicans. However, they did give the single most valuable tip in securing employment illegally in Fort Lauderdale. The yachts. Unbeknown to us at that stage, Fort Lauderdale was a yachting paradise. They suggested approaching the yachting fraternity for work; not only would it be much better paid, but it would also be fun with the potential for travel. We drove back to the beach in Fort Lauderdale where we would sleep for the next week, with heavy hearts. Neither Daniel nor I had the first clue about yachts, boats or anything that involved water outside having a bath.

The next morning, we sat in the van smoking, trying to come up with an approach. We thought the situation was hopeless. We knew nothing about this industry, but we had met some of the yachting crew types a few weeks back. They were a strange breed, hardy and impassioned with the lifestyle; most importantly, they had credibility, some of them had sailed from Auckland and the like.

My dad used to own a sailing boat, and every weekend, he would drive himself and me to a most pathetic lake, where the boat was stored. We would spend the whole morning rigging the thing up, then when it came to sailing, I was always told to stay onshore as it was too dangerous. I was a kid at the time. This was the closest I had come to any sailing. Eventually, he had to sell it to buy a new washing machine, the irony was not lost on me, but I was grateful to not have to see that miserable lake again. Eventually, we decided the best way forward would be to hang out in the yachting bars and chat with the guys already doing this work to see what advice, if any they could dispense. And that night, that's exactly what we did.

After traversing a few of the many yachting joints on the main strip, we ended up sitting next to a guy from the UK. He looked the part, and we decided to approach him and after a polite introduction and a drink. He gave us all the information we needed. He broke it down for us in bullet points. We sat there and dutifully took notes, asking the odd question for clarification. He was almost inspirational, believing we could wing it if we had the courage. We left that evening with a solid plan and far more confidence that this might work. We only

47

needed it to work for a couple of weeks; this was not a career choice.

The next day, we drove to JCPenny, and with the last of our cash and my credit card, we shopped for clothes. We needed to look like sailors; we bought special deck friendly shoes, beige pleated frat boy shorts and a few brightly coloured polo neck shirts. Our transformation had begun. We set up a voicemail box to be able to receive calls. The next stop was Atlantic University, where we snuck into their library pretending to be students and spent a few hours on their computers banging our fake sailing resumes and business cards complete with our newly setup voicemail box number. After saving them to disk, we left and headed to the local Kinkos to print and cut the cards. We celebrated the morning's achievement by sharing a toxic burger meal from yet another faceless fast-food joint.

The next few days were spent pounding the pavement so to speak, by driving to different harbours in and around the greater Fort Lauderdale area, trying to distribute our business cards. We were mightily frustrated by the fact that these areas required passes to gain access; you needed a reason to be there, as they were, for obvious reasons, high-security areas with restricted access. Most times, we were not able to make it through the front gate. Thus, we had to settle with pinning our cards on the local notice boards and dropping our CVs off at the local yachting recruitment shops. The competition was fierce, and we knew we were fake, which took its psychological toll. The days went by slowly. To save fuel, driving was restricted to only the essential trips, mainly those that required looking for work. We didn't have much to do with our time except sit on the beach and periodically check in with our voicemail box. To this day, we never actually received a message. Somehow, we kept it together; we always seemed to have money for cigarettes, which went a long way to pacify the situation. We played music, we read and entered into long discussions, each somehow reinforcing that our decision made that day in Daniel's mother's kitchen was still the right decision. I was adamant I would never ask my parents for help. I would not fail, and going cap in hand to my parents would constitute failure. I doubt they even had the means to be honest. Daniel agreed, albeit his family was very well off compared to my own. At this stage, he was also pining for Neelen; he seemed to have fallen quite in love with her. I couldn't blame him.

It was during this time that I noticed a change in myself. I dismissed it at first, but my actions over the past weeks and mental steadfastness alluded to the fact that I had graduated of sorts. I had become quite resourceful, hard and almost ruthless. I relished the fact; it had been one of my goals. In contrast, Daniel had become softer, mainly due to his longing for this girl; it was as if we had swapped roles. This was evident in the fact he had unwittingly become the de facto diver, albeit he didn't have a license, whereas I had become the brains and navigator. It had been different at the start of the trip. The other thing that had changed was that we had become friends and would remain so for the rest of our lives.

It wasn't long afterward whilst out placing our resumes and business cards at some of the crewing agencies dotted around the city that we struck gold. I had double-parked the van. I still did some of the driving, especially around town, whilst Daniel had run into an agency that we had circled as one we had yet to leave details with. After a few minutes,

Daniel jumped in the van sporting an excited grin. As he shut the door, he shoved an advert he had ripped off the notice board in my face and exclaimed, "LOOK!" I was in shock; was I dreaming? Before my eyes was an advert that read: Two experienced sailors required, South African's preferred! with contact details attached. I had to look twice before I could even formulate a reply. We floored the van to the nearest payphone and made the call. A southern accent answered, and after an exchange of pleasantries and a short chat, we had secured an interview for that afternoon at a local harbour with Ken. We nervously spent the rest of the morning showering and shaving on the beach and mentally preparing for our first crewing interview. We had no idea what to expect; we just decided to go with the flow, but we were just grateful for the opportunity which seemed almost divine.

On arriving, we were met by a man in his mid-50s, we presumed Ken; he greeted us politely and beckoned for us to come aboard. This was the first time in my life I had ever set foot on a yacht of any type. Little did I know at that stage it wasn't just any yacht. I would soon learn just how special this vessel was. We were invited to take a seat in the sunny cabin; it seemed so bourgeois to me at that time. As we apprehensively readied for the interview, I noticed something familiar displayed on a wall further in the cabin: a picture of Table Mountain. There was a South African connection here, and we didn't have to wait long for it to be revealed. Right as the interview got started a woman also in her mid-50s appeared. "Are these our South African sailors?" she exclaimed in a rather posh Capetonian accent. She was Ken's wife, Hazel Beckman. The interview proceeded well; it consisted mostly of them telling their story of how they had come to own this yacht and the good experience they had had on their journey so far with various South Africa crew they had hired; there was also a fair bit of reminiscing about Cape Town. Our experience as written on our fake resumes was never actually questioned; however, Ken having previously owned an electronics company knew very well the importance of a tech test, to weed out the pros from the chaff so to speak. Before long, he had presented me with a rope and was calling out different knot types to be demonstrated on the fly. Knot demonstration requests were interspersed with navigation questions. Daniel looked on in amazement, as I was able to almost blindly tie bowlines and sheepshanks whilst answering the navigation theory. During my young teenage years, I had been a fervent scout, one of the youngest in the country to have achieved their Springbok colours. This experience more than prepared me for this simple test and allowed us to seal the deal. We were hired on the spot and asked to start the next morning; 80 USD a day, full board and lodging with a 2,000-mile sail ahead of us. We drove back to our beach parking that evening, feeling like kings. Although we had worked together to achieve this, this had largely been my doing: my contacts, my modus operandi and my skills had saved us; my confidence was at an all-time high.

Early next morning, we said goodbye to the beach parking that had been our home for the last few weeks and drove to the harbour to start our first day's work as a yachting crew. Akin to how we had dressed for our interview the day before we had darned our JCPenny frat-boy attire, this was to be our pseudo uniform for the days ahead.

During the interview the previous day, it had been made known to us that the yacht already had a seasoned crew member onboard. Kyle, a New Zealander who had formed part of a crew that had sailed from Auckland to Florida a few months back. Both Daniel and I knew that to survive this job, we would have to befriend Kyle and learn as much from him as possible. This we decided was going to be our priority. Almost as if inferred, it was explained to us that he was second in command after Ken; this suited us fine. The first few days were spent doing rather menial work; our tasks included sanding and painting the bilges, accompanying the Beckmans on shopping trips to provision the yacht for its imminent sailing, loading stuff, cleaning, etc. By now, we lived on the yacht. We shared a four-bed cabin with Kyle; our workdays started at 8 and ended at 6. All our meals were provisioned and cooked by Hazel, and we got paid weekly in cash. There were a few simple rules: from 6 in the evening to 8 in the morning, we could do what we wanted, where we wanted, as long as we were ready on deck for work at 8; secondly, we were to do what was asked well. Our relationship with Kyle blossomed into a full-blown friendship; it didn't take long for him to notice that we were not as experienced as we purported to be. He seemed to respect our courage and endeavoured to take us under his wing. We quickly became inseparable, and through him, we met the antipodean yachting diaspora based in Fort Lauderdale, which had the compounding effect of immersing us in the lifestyle.

We were grateful for those initial pre-sail days moored in Fort Lauderdale. It gave us time to learn whilst replenishing some of our cash flow. As our sail date approached, we needed to figure out what to do with our van; we would be in Connecticut in a week or so. Daniel and I decided to leave it at the office of the South African thatching company that we had met up a few weeks before. They seemed happy to help; thus, a day or two before setting sail, we packed the van and drove it back to the nondescript industrial area, where the thatching company was based. The van had become part of our identity, and we were sad and worried about leaving it. We had no idea what was going to happen to us and even less idea of when we would be reunited again. We diligently detached and battery-locked it, and bode it farewell.

For every day after us having joined the yacht Shearwater as crew, the city had been set ablaze by the annual Fort Lauderdale air show. I had been to air shows back home on a few occasions, but this was in a league all of its own. The vantage point we enjoyed working off coast only added to the surreality of the experience. To our flank, a fleet of Arleigh Burke-class destroyers cut a majestic sight on the horizon. Overhead, it seemed like some sort of high-altitude Formula One was ensuing. We seemed to be strategically located at the start of the flyby. Overhead, each of the demonstration teams would do a few low altitude loops, before opening up the fuel taps then and with full afterburner break the sound barrier down the beach, where Joe Public was waiting. It was a total show of confidence. The first Gulf War was long since over and won. Netscape had just IPO'd a year earlier and Clinton was a favourite to get re-elected. The country was riding high; we embraced the energy. Two days into the air show, rather ominously, ValueJet flight 592 crashed into the Everglades after taking off from Miami airport; all 110 lives were lost. It was May 11, 1996. The very next day, we set sail.

Mystic

The Fort Lauderdale skyline slowly faded away into obscurity as we sailed ever closer to the Gulf Stream; this natural occurring northbound current, as we learned, was to be our pseudo catapult up the coast and away from the searing heat, which was going to be brought to bear on the sunshine state during the summer. Getting our sea legs didn't take too long; mind you, the sea was as calm as a swimming pool that day and, luckily, would remain like that for most of the trip. Lady luck was going to smile on us once more as we soon learned that the sailing conditions were less than ideal for a conventional sail; thus, we were left with no choice but use the engine to propel us. Moreover, it seemed this was likely to remain the case for the best part of the trip. The consequence of this meant there was no requirement to display our non-existing sailing skills; it also meant more leisure time just sitting around on the yacht, getting paid. After a few hours, we were surrounded by the ocean; at first, it felt liberating and freeing, but then it became almost claustrophobic. The yacht was more than just a luxury status item now; it had transformed into our life support system. We were dependent on it for survival. The rest of the day was spent completing the chores we had started in port and holding debrief sessions with Kyle to get to grips with some of the finer points of sailing.

Later that evening, after our first dinner, we were briefed of the night shift duties, which would be needed to prevent a collision with other vessels. The route we were taking would traverse one of the busiest shipping routes in the world. We had seen evidence of this during the day; vessels ranging from other yachts to mega container ships would dot in and out of our radar, like Pacman. Daniel, Kyle and I would each get two shifts of two hours each; this would be required for the duration of the sail. My experience as a cadet during my high school years had wisely taught me to volunteer for the first and last shifts, as this guaranteed the best sleep. Cadets were a kinda enforced school pre-army that was used by the then government as a conduit to actual conscription, so much so during my last three years in high school, I had to often dress in the drab apartheid military uniform and attend camps to hone my fighting skills. Many a night would you have found me on forced guard duty brandishing an automatic weapon, with no bullets, guarding against an existential threat, which to this day I have yet to encounter.

Sitting alone that first night under the stars with my one hand on the helm and my eyes darting between the GPS and Radar screens, it dawned on me just how unqualified for the job I was. Down below were four lives that depended on me keeping us from colliding with a super tanker. The bigger ships would totally ignore you and you would just need to steer away; luckily, they appeared large on the screen. The smaller vessels would often entertain me with chat on the radio; this broke the boredom, especially on the quieter nights. I remember one surreal morning whilst on last shift, the US coast guard radioed into me from a reconnaissance aircraft above; they were on routine patrol looking for shipments of drugs and illegals. After radioing back our call sign, they recognised the ship for what is a US floating heritage and proceeded to have a ten-minute discussion with me bordering on the patriotic. The irony of them having unleashed a monologue about keeping the country safe from illegals wasn't lost on me, an illegal worker myself.

The next five days proceeded rather uneventfully; we let the Gulf Stream do most of the work, pushing us slowly up the coast. The few dole drums we did experience were countered by turning on the diesel engine for a few hours. There was no rush, albeit we did have a deadline, as we had booked a dry dock in New London for the following week. Apart from our daily chores, which revolved basic maintenance duties, we would while our time away on deck taking in the vastness of the ocean. Oftentimes, we would be accompanied by a school of dolphins; they would surround the vessel and take turns fearlessly diving in front of the ship's bow. The ease with which they moved was a total personification of freedom; their almost daily appearance seemed to embolden me to further break the societal chains that had been wrapped around me under the guise of the church, family and a repressive schooling system. At this stage, going back was not an option.

Arriving in Mystic after a full five days at sea brought with it a feeling of relief and angst. It was great to be back on dry land, but the knowledge that the real work had yet to begin filled us with dread; we had but a few weeks to get the yacht certified. By now, it had become obvious that our skills were not commensurate with that of an experienced crew hand.

This had started to subtly reveal itself with the deterioration in the relationship between the Beckmans and us. This was especially pertinent in Hazel and Daniel's interactions. Oftentimes there had been pseudo arguments and misunderstanding concerning assignments. I too had let the ball drop several times. The honeymoon was definitely over. We realised that this was not going to last very long, but we had to keep going as long as we could for the sake of our self-preservation.

That evening after work, Daniel and I decided to get some distance from the yacht and explore the town. It felt like we had arrived on a movie set reminiscent of an episode of the twilight zone. It sported all the trappings of a small harbour town one would expect of the area; it was charming, quaint and very upmarket. However, it also seemed to have a dark side. Before long, we found ourselves at one of the trendy coffee shops that served coffee from industrial-size thermos flasks in about 20 different flavours. This, like many places, we had been too on our trip, seemed to be full of disillusioned teenagers, all looking for an escape from the drudgery of their daily lives. These coffee shops seemed to be the go-to place from which to hatch more malevolent plans that would inevitably involve contraband. They would become our de facto hangouts during the subsequent evenings; we would often find ourselves the centre of attention and would use this to fully exploit the situation to our mischievous ends, whether to seduce, acquire drugs, alcohol or all three. Almost without fail, we would be stopped and questioned on a return to the harbour. The police countrywide seemed to have an innate prejudice against guys with long hair. Not uniquely American, as I had experienced this regularly back in South

Africa, seemingly anything different caused them anxiety. We were always polite, co-operative and very understanding of their polarised small-mindedness.

The plan insofar as it pertained to the Beckmans was simple, ready the yacht to be US coast guard certified then charter it out for corporate functions and weddings, etc. This would require no small maintenance effort to get the yacht shipshape and its papers in order. Not long after we arrived in Mystic, we set sail for a larger port with dry dock facilities in New London. After the herculean task of getting the yacht into the dry dock, which took the best part of a morning, we set about scraping, sanding and painting. It was back-breaking work; the dry dock had been booked for a fixed period; thus, the pressure was on to complete the work. The situation did nothing to alleviate the now almost toxic relationship between us and the Beckmans. We knew our days were numbered and expected to be let go soon.

The honeymoon of the sail had long since evaporated. The work routine now prevailed; however, our time in Connecticut wasn't without a few serendipitous experiences. One evening, as we were packing up for the evening, we were approached by a group of young kids around our age. They explained they had recently procured a yacht and wanted an expert opinion on what would be needed to get it ready for a circumnavigation. Having been a rather obvious sight over the past few days working high up in the dry dock, we seemed to have the credibility they were looking for. They beckoned for us to follow them to another part of the dockyard to inspect their vessel. To our surprise, we found a rusted floating hull, minus all the trappings that you would expect from a vessel earmarked for a world sailing. What they lacked in a yacht they more than made up for in enthusiasm. We promised to help as much as we could but convinced them to join us getting drunk that night in a local bar. The next day hungover, we set sail for Mystic; we never saw those kids again.

After our arrival back in Mystic, we were rather unceremoniously fired. I remember it clearly; we were paid up and given an hour to pack our belongings. Daniel and I soon switched back into survival mode and quickly set about organising our next move. We were conscious we were 1,400 miles away from our van, but at least we had improved our cash flow. We decided it best to buy two Amtrak tickets back to NYC and crash with Jenny until we could figure out the best way to get to Florida. At this stage, we acted like two pros working in unison to turn the situation around. On calling Amtrak to enquire about the two tickets back to NYC, our trip took another unexpected turn. After a few minutes on the call, the customer service representative made it clear what a pleasure it was to hear a foreign accent that was not Mexican; moreover, he went out of his way to get us a great deal. After hanging up, I had bought two 15-day Amtrak passes covering Maine to Louisiana for less than a single ticket to NYC.

Ken drove us to the Amtrak station, shook our hands and sped off. The train back to NYC that evening was filled with young men and women in smart naval uniforms. I suspected they were all cadets in training going home for the weekend. Their neat, disciplined, controlled appearance in total juxtaposition to ourselves: longhaired, dishevelled and living by our wits. A part of me envied them; they didn't seem to need to worry about the future or their next meal, their mundane routine seemed so safe. Then I just thought about the dolphins swimming past us a few days earlier and smiled:

I was free. The parents, the old school and the old country had no jurisdiction over me anymore. I was beginning to think differently, it would remain like this for the rest of my life.

It's a few short hours from New London to NYC. The scenery on offer as we snaked our way down to New York seemed majestic and puritanical; it added to our feeling that our trip was about to take another twist. We were happy to be away from the yachting world. It had been a great experience; however, we had a road trip to finish and we now had the funds in hand. Arriving in Penn station later that evening felt like a homecoming. I always felt like I was on cocaine in that city. My energy levels were high at the best of times; in NYC, they went through the roof. We had made contact with Jenny in New England and had arranged to rendezvous at the station after her work and catch the Subway back to Queens. Whilst waiting for her to arrive, we ran into a young nerdy-looking guy kicking his heels waiting for his own rendezvous. Before long, he was describing this concept of hitching rides on empty seats of airliners between Europe and the US. Intrigued by this concept, we got into details of how this might work; moreover, this led to an intriguing discussion on the tantalising prospect of exploring Europe, especially the recently opened Eastern Europe. It was a timely discussion as our time in the US was coming to end; we had a month left on our visa. We parted after swapping contacts and a few notes about the air-hitching idea.

Amtrak

It had been a little over three and half weeks since we had left NYC for the allure of Spring Break; however, on reuniting with Jenny that evening and sharing our story with her on the Subway home, it felt like a lifetime had passed. Whilst nothing in her life had changed, her daily commute to and from the city, interspersed with a few social events, had been her mainstay. We had gone broke, reinvented ourselves as sailors, made new contacts, crewed a yacht 1,400 miles, returned to positive cash flow and gotten fired.

If nothing else, it was a story worth telling and she hung on our every word that evening.

The next few days were spent reacquainting ourselves with our favourite bagel shops, whilst entertaining discussions about our next move. We had three weeks or so before our visa was up. We had enough money to survive; however, we needed to sell the van to secure funding for an air ticket out the country. We had return air tickets in hand; however, neither of us were going back to Johannesburg. Going home would constitute failure at every level.

It was June 1996, and the book, The Celestine Prophecy, had been published just three years before. I noticed it had appeared large in several bookshops that I had frequented during my time in the country. I had also noticed it in full view on the table in Jenny's flat on our stay previously. I was sceptical when it came to anything spiritual; 17 years of Catholicism had done much irreparable damage that the drugs were only starting to undo; thus, at the time, I thought nothing of it and never gave it a second glance. During those few days on our return from Mystic, I decided to pick it up and give it a read. To this day, I can't say it was a life-changing experience by any means, but it was symbolic, as it was the first time I had allowed myself the opportunity to explore something new, an alternative to what had been prescribed to me. The first chapter about synchronicity had me replay the last few months and connect the dots backward. This was my first foray into self-awareness, something I had not known was even possible. For most of my life, I had never been permitted to think anything that ran contrary to the dogma of the church and state. The experience gave me a new insight: I had been looking for my freedom solely in the construct of the physical world. Freedom is not solely a physical construct or lack thereof; it's also a state of awareness. This is why I was never satisfied with the destination; as soon I would arrive somewhere, I immediately wanted to leave. To me, my restlessness was a symptom of my lack of awareness. My journey into self-awareness might have started in NYC, summer 1996, but continues still today.

Much like the last time when living with Jenny in Queens, Daniel and I spent most of our time apart, sharing only our mornings at our local bagel shop and then again our evenings on the bank of the Hudson River overlooking the mighty NYC skyline slowly sinking under the setting sun whilst drinking beer. Our beer bottles would be wrapped in this quintessential brown paper packet as required by legacy prohibition laws, a most inauthentic attempt at covering supposed immorality, if there was ever one. I metaphorically linked this to my own life and how it had until that point been papered over to be respectable for society's whims.

It was on one of these evenings sitting on the embankment that we firmed up the plan for the next few weeks. Daniel was missing Neleen so much that he decided to take the Amtrak to Sycryse and visit her; they had already telephonically agreed to this. I would come to understand this feeling of missing someone deeply in my later years. Nothing can stop the pain; no amount of forced distractions or the like works for very long. You just need to see the person. I planned to exploit the 15-day Amtrak pass all the way to New Orleans. It was agreed that we would meet in 1.5 weeks at the Amtrak Station in Fort Lauderdale, to pick up the van and drive her back to NYC. This would give us about 1.5 weeks to sell it and get out of the country before our visa expired. Optimistic at best, foolhardy at worst.

The next morning, I packed my backpack and took the subway to Penn Station, where I boarded an Amtrak bound for Atlanta. I was travelling alone for the first time since we had left Johannesburg. I felt nervous but completely emancipated at the thought of embarking solo. Looking back now, it was probably the least risky time to take the step with the journey itself presenting no real challenges at all; however, it still felt like my Rubicon moment.

Peering out the window of the train that morning, seeing the ubiquitous Twin Towers slowly disappearing into the distance, it felt strange to not be driving on the now all too familiar turnpikes and interstates. The US railroads seemed rather neglected when compared to the road system. It was a well-known fact that the country prized the car over any form of public transport. This was true of my own country where we had foolishly put the tram in the museum in the '70s and completely bought into the car culture. In that respect, it felt great to be taking in the country from a very different perspective.

Boarding a long-distance Amtrak train in 1996 felt akin to stepping back in time. It was almost comical. The uniforms the crew wore seemed remnant of the 1950s; their-larger-than-life brightly coloured lapels and caps seemed to be only matched by their overly animated demeanour. They proved a welcome distraction from the sometimes-laborious landscape passing by outside. I settled in with a book and tried to relax; it was going to be a long 18 hours before Atlanta. I didn't have the money for a sleeper and thus had to be happy with the standard Amtrak seat.

A little while later, I found myself in the dining car ordering alcohol to numb the boredom. The carriage was brimming with guests and thus I found myself sharing a table with a motley crew of mad individuals. Two individuals in particular, albeit being unrelated, seemed to be drawn to me: one, a woman in her 40s, well-oiled even at this early stage of the trip and a nerdy-looking clean-cut guy in his late 20s. The woman initially took centre stage with her hard-luck story revolving around being beaten to a pulp by her husband. As the story unfolded in its gruesome detail, it was established that she was on her way back to her family in Atlanta to escape the violence. If there was any doubt about the authenticity of her tale, it was put paid to by the bruises she brandished, most notably her black swollen eye. Seemingly, this was not the first time she had been through this. We sat there for hours talking and drinking, interrupted only by the entertaining flamboyantly dressed crew offering us refills.

The nerdy guy had his own story, albeit to this day, I am not sure how believable it was. He had been given his full sleeper Amtrak ticket by his family as a gift for being accepted at some university in Georgia. However, his stories centred around being an ex-soldier that had spent time in Lebanon during the civil war. The stories were of stoic bravado and totally entertaining. Other crazies darted in and out of our sphere, to add to the flavour of the night until such time we couldn't drink anymore. It was at this point the battered woman managed to manipulate the sleeper away from the nerdy ex-soldier; I collapsed on my seat and quickly fell asleep.

The next morning as we rolled into Atlanta Station, incidentally the host of the summer Olympics in a few months, I considered the state of the station facilities and concluded they weren't expecting many visitors to be arriving by rail. Crude at best.

On disembarking, I regrouped with the characters from the previous day, and together, we set off to a local diner to grab some breakfast. Upon sitting and ordering, we started to discuss our individual plans for the day. Suddenly, out of nowhere in violent contrast to the atmosphere in the establishment, in barges, a tall scrawny long-faced bloke, cowboy hat in hand, walked up to our table and manhandled the battered woman off her seat and frogmarched her out whilst screaming all sorts of profanities. Shocked, I just sat there in disbelief. I and all in the diner looked on as a large pickup truck hurriedly drove out the parking lot.

During breakfast, I discussed with the surviving character, the nerdy ex-soldier, that I planned to walk to a bohemian suburb not far from the centre and explore what it had to offer. To my surprise, he followed me like a puppy dog for the rest of the day. Together we walked past Martin Luther King's house and onto little five points, the suburb in question. The iconic house seemed as expected, so humble, in relation to the effect the man had had on the history of the country, but then compared to Nelson's Mandela's place, a shack in a Johannesburg township, total luxury. On arriving, we found a coffee shop that seemed overrun with the typical runaway American teenagers and their accompanying dogs. I had met many of these people throughout my journey, all kids around the same age as me, all with similar dreams for something more meaningful, more authentic. Most of them had the same narrative, solving the problem by physically moving somewhere, the most common destination being California. Somehow California had captured the imagination of these kids. Their discussions reminded me of my own back in January whilst frequenting the doors. I tried my best to inspire them, but most of the time, they had given into sloth and had become bogged down in the dream rather than taking any action. After a while, I managed to lose my entourage and was happy about it. Atlanta was an uninspiring city in 1996, bland and sprawling. I hadn't planned on staying more than 48 hours and soon made my way to a local youth hostel for the night. The next day, I spent exploring the Olympic city; the day after, I boarded my train for New Orleans.

I arrived in New Orleans late that evening after a rather uneventful trip spent reading and peering out the window, taking in the changing landscape. The easy-going vibe the city is world-renowned for hit me as soon as I exited the station. I had no plan; all I knew is that I needed to be back to catch my train the next evening to be on time for the planned meetup with Daniel in Fort Lauderdale. After a short stop to get my bearings, I donned my backpack and headed straight for the famous Bourbon Street. The city was littered with weirdo's and tourists, each seemingly at ease with each other; it struck a chord with me. I felt it the least judgmental city I had been to in the USA, and it reminded me a little of Woodstock in Cape Town, one of the few places people of all races were comfortable together in South Africa. After taking in the sights, I headed to a park near the coast to chill out and plan my evening further.

As I sat and leaned back on my pack a little while later, I noticed the park was alive with energy, and all around me were young people, playing bongo drums, juggling and even chanting. The atmosphere was reminiscent of what I read about in books describing the then scene on islands dotted around Southeast Asia, which, in 1996, had become a backpacking hotspot for European and Antipodean youngsters looking to get away for a gap year. After taking in my surroundings, I decided to join a few groups. The people were a mix of the same type of characters I had met on my trip thus far, broadly made up of the young adults that had got lost in the sloth of their dreams of finding a better life, not unlike the group I had run into a few days earlier in Atlanta, interspersed with a few naval seamen who had run away to join the navy for much the same reason the previous group had chosen to escape. However, they were now subjected to stringent routines and laborious toilet cleaning duties that came with being a non-commissioned officer. Then there were the tourists, people with mostly vanilla lives, peering in for a few hours but safe in their attachment to their spreadsheet routines that waited for them back at their offices, universities or churches.

It wasn't long before I met a group of friends, three in number: two girls and a guy, all around 16 from Lafayette, a town about two hours away up the coast. Strangely enough, they were augmented by another guy much older, who like me had also just met them. He was from somewhere in Texas and seemed to blow his trumpet at every chance he got. Somehow, we were all drawn together that night, so in the spirit of synchronicity, I joined them for an adventure in New Orleans. That evening started innocently enough, drinking and enjoying the comings and goings around us, but before long, I found myself smitten with the one girl, Charlotte. Her pitch-black long hair, pale skin, nymph body and dreamy southern accent had me hooked in no time, notwithstanding the age difference, which I didn't care about. Anyway, kids seemed to grow up much faster in the USA than where I came from, at least quicker than I had; she was perfect.

The night took on a sultry, adventurous energy that took all of us from the park to the blues clubs in Bourbon Street, down the dark streets of the city's business sector, back up to the clubs then eventually back to the park. At about 5 in the morning, inebriated and high, we collapsed in a heap on a bench in full view of a brightly lit US naval warship. It wasn't long before we lost our brave, larger-than-life Texan to his inflated ego, which he had propped by proving how much more he could drink than the rest of us. It was at that point that things took a turn for the more sinister. On noticing the slumbering Texan, the girls proceeded to rob him of his money, by slowly massaging his wallet from his back pocket and removing his cash, then slipping it back. I looked on in horror as it transpired in slow motion in front of my eyes. After this, they turned to me and rather nonchalantly asked if I wanted to go to Tony's for coffee. Against my better judgment, I said yes.

Not long after I was in the backseat of their car, being driven out of the city deep into Mark Twain's Huckleberry Finn County. I had naively thought Tony's was a diner in town. As we drove over the many cantilever bridges connecting the city to the rest of the swampy state, I did my best to keep calm. It wasn't the first time I had made a foolhardy decision because of a girl, and it wasn't to be my last either. Eerily, nobody spoke on the drive.

After 20 minutes of driving, we pulled off the tar road and onto a dirt track. We followed this for a few minutes and stopped at a boardwalk, which stretched out over a swampy lake. Seemingly a ritual for them, they wanted to take in the sunrise; they got out, me in tow. I was fearfully keeping my distance. Nearing the edge of the boardwalk, I could see the whole lake was infested with alligators; one, in particular, caught my attention, a dead corpse floating on its back riddled with maggots. It was a sunrise like no other for me; thankfully, after we finished sharing a cigarette, we piled back into the car and drove off further into swamp country.

After about an hour, we came to a stop outside a wooden house in the middle of some trees. By now, I realised that Tony was a friend of theirs and not a coffee shop. Walking into the kitchen that morning reminded me a little of my grandmother's kitchen, bland and laden with heavy bars on the window. In the corner at the table sat an old man eating what looked like porridge with a spoon. I distinctly remember him having no teeth. We shuffled passed, saying nothing and made our way into the back room. The room was filled with confederate flags and other icons of a different era; this sent chills up my spine.

It wasn't long before the enigma himself appeared like our apparition from Lourdes. Gun in hand, he embraced everybody and politely greeted me. I was then subjected to a lecture on the evils of government and was given an idiot's guide to libertarianism. I distinctly remember him asking me what the best country in the world was. I wasn't gonna lie; it wasn't South Africa, or somewhere in Europe. After this, we all collapsed on the floor and watched reruns of cops until we all fell asleep.

I awoke a few hours later in a panic. I had a train to catch that evening. I had to meet Daniel, drive the van back to NYC, sell the thing and get out of the country before my visa expired. I had no idea where I was, somewhere in some swamp in a hut with a lot of guns and weird flags. Having largely sobered up now, I gently woke Charlotte and politely explained my dilemma. I was totally at her mercy; somehow, this lack of control added spice to the situation. Within minutes, this same girl who had robbed somebody a few hours earlier was racing me back to New Orleans as if her life depended on it. The swamped raced by to the sound of Nine Inch Nails at top volume. I've been a fan of that band ever since.

We arrived with 15 minutes to spare. I kissed her goodbye with her contact details in hand and hoofed it to my train. As I collapsed in my seat, out of breath, I watched the city go by in an almost ebb and flow like motion. My incandescent feelings for New Orleans were slowly being replaced by the business at hand. Next stop, Fort Lauderdale.

Disembarking the train at the Amtrak Station in Fort Lauderdale the next afternoon, I found Daniel already waiting for me on the platform. Relieved that we had both made it as agreed, we were notably happy to see each other. The days apart had done our relationship good, and I was anxious to hear how it had gone with Neleen up in Syracuse; however, that would have to wait till later. After a short taxi ride to the outskirts of the city, we were soon reunited with our van; this after a hiatus of close to a month but what felt like a year. We quickly set about connecting the battery and to our relief, the engine started on at first attempt. Ten minutes later, we were cruising at 55 miles an hour up the I-95, a road we knew like the back of our hands now.

Exit

We didn't have the luxury of time on our side anymore; we also had very little margin for error, and again, we were being faced with our old nemesis, the cash flow situation, albeit not as dire as it had been a month ago. For the most part, Daniel had supplemented his cash flow with two stolen credit cards he had lifted from customers in the high-end restaurant he had worked in whilst still in Johannesburg. Thinking back, I was complicit in this crime, as I simply turned a blind eye whenever he used them; moreover, I had by implication benefitted. We had a simple system of sharing the costs; we split everything down the line, except for the van where I was disproportionately invested to the tune of 70 cents on the dollar. Not long after we had left Fort Lauderdale, we pulled into a service station in Orlando to refuel and replenish supplies for the journey ahead. It was Daniel's turn to pay. His normal modus operandi was to attempt to pay with one of the hot cards, holding the cash in hand in case something went wrong. For the most part due to the way cards were pre-authorised those days, manually, this worked. In the few situations where it had failed, he was able to get away with it using the excuse of it being a foreign card and handing over the cash. After what seemed an unusually long time to facilitate the purchase of the fuel, without warning, I saw Daniel making a dash for it in the rear-view mirror, commanding me to drive; shocked, I turned the key and slipped the van into 'drive'. By this time, he had joined me in the cabin, holding the van's number plate, which he had ripped off in the vain hope of concealing our identity. In what seemed like a scene straight out of 'Thelma and Louise', we sped off down the road, panicked, shocked and laughing. I never heard the details of what happened inside that service station and I was happy with that. A few minutes later, we were back on the Interstate and heading for NYC.

As usual, we were going to do the trip without stopping taking turns throughout the night. At some point during the evening, we got to exchange our experiences over the past week whilst travelling. Seemingly, it hadn't gone that well in Syracuse with Neleen. He had stayed with her in her parents' house; however, he had seemingly been side-lined whilst there. I tried to explain to him that the holiday fling had served a greater purpose by introducing us to Jenny, who had not only become a good friend but had saved us twice and was going to do it for the third time. For the most part, the rest of the trip was uneventful; the I-95 had become as familiar as my old commute to work, and it seemed as if the van knew where to go without even needing to be steered.

That morning, about 300 miles outside of NYC, we stopped off at one of those soulless fast-food places to grab a high-calorie toxic breakfast, to see us through to our destination. Most of these places required me to dumb down in order just to survive the experience. My almost near-daily ritual of visiting these places taught me that the people working on the front lines of customer service were not comfortable with nuance. Any challenge or attempt at discourse insofar, it came to the menu or the rules were ritually met with the menu options being repeated or a blanket silence. It was like I was having a discussion with a flow chart. To be honest, this attitude wasn't localised to fast-food establishments. I had routinely run into this at every level. If Americans were a character in Frank Baum's Wizard of Oz, they would be the TIN man, needing a heart or more specifically a soul. I had by that stage mentally checked out of the country and was looking forward to the escape.

We arrived in NYC late that morning, exhausted and slightly intimidated by the challenges that lay ahead. Our first priority was to shift the van. At this stage, we had a week and a half left on our visa. Staying with Jenny was also going to be complicated, as in a few days Neleen would be coming to stay, as she had business in the city. This was going to have a psychological effect on Daniel, just when I needed him to be on form.

We decided the best thing was to take out an advert in the New York Times classified section using our number we had set up in Florida whilst searching for work a few weeks back. By this stage, we had also made acquaintance with most of the people that lived on Jenny's street in Queens and used them to spread the word. We would religiously check the voicemail every hour or so for any interest. Initially, we had some, but they all for one or another reason seemed to lose interest once they had us follow up with a call. The rest of the time we tried to decide what our next move would be. The prospect of not knowing where in the world we would be the following week was as intimidating as it was enthralling and we couldn't help being gratuitous for the luxuries position we found ourselves in. The morning Neleen arrived, I decided to use my remaining Amtrak ticket to go visit Boston, both to get away from the impending drama and to visit the city properly. We had driven through on our initial journey; however, the weather had been awful and as such had not spent much time exploring. I arrived in Boston early on a Saturday morning, and after spending some time meandering around its open spaces and taking in its skyline, I decided to make my way to Cambridge, the home of the famous Harvard University.

I still remember her sitting there in the middle of Harvard Square, dressed alternatively, big fly glasses, Dr Martens and sporting a bob of fine mousy brown hair. I sat for a minute, placed my backpack down and took in the environment. All around there were artists and exhibitionists punting their talents. People from all walks of life seemed to congregate here. I made sure to direct my gaze at her through a group of jugglers thus not to appear to be staring. The wind was blowing and I remember this caused her hair to flutter around her soft almond-shaped face; this only increased my intrigue; I could bear it no more. I walked over, touched her on the shoulder and commented on the dexterity of the jugglers which had up until that moment had her fixated. "Oh hello," she said in a forced British accent as if to tease me.

An hour later, we were walking hand in hand down the embankment of the Charles River. It was a beautiful afternoon. Boston had, within a short space of five hours, been transformed from a cold stark Amtrak Station to a beautiful romantic paradise. Our walking would be interspersed by moments of intense discussions of our immediate environment, each discussion and attempt at gaining further insight into our respective personalities. We were after all perfect strangers from completely opposite sides of the world.

That evening to my delight, both because I had nowhere to stay and because I was smitten, she invited me to her home. She lived with her mother, a short corpulent woman who seemed to be carrying an emotional sadness. Pleasant enough but understandable wary of this uninvited foreigner her daughter had brought home. I tried to allay her mother's fears through a constructive discussion about myself, she was typically American, but I took a liking to her, she felt it and reacted with kindness. Kim and I spent the rest of the night in her converted attic bedroom listening to music, discussing theatre, art and our favourite authors. She had a broad interest in music and for her age, only 16 at the time, she was very well read. Totally different in persona to Charlotte, the girl I had met just a week before in New Orleans, Kim, less vivacious than Charlotte, had a heaviness to her, which I interpreted as depth. That night, I learned that a few months back she, with the sanction of her psychologist, had dropped out of school, temporarily due to personal circumstances. I had always been attracted to this type: the dark, closed and broody personalities, and by this stage in her loft, I was hooked. We communicated that evening via music, stories and poetry we had each written until we fell asleep.

The next day, she took me to Artists for Humanity, a type of outreach program that promotes talented teenage artists and assists with funding, etc. This she explained is where she spent most of her days: painting and drawing and developing her talent. The place was half studio and half gallery. I hadn't quite seen anything like this before in my life. South Africa had never championed the arts, never mind providing funding for facilities that encouraged young prospective artists from struggling backgrounds. South Africa was more interested in censoring art. The arts had always been seen as threatening to the previous regime.

As she guided me around the facilities and showed me her work, I met many of her fellow artists from all over Boston, including the curators who ran the programme. Afterwards, I took us to lunch in the city at a place she recommended, and we spent the rest of the afternoon in each other's arms sitting in one of the many small parks dotted in and around the city. That evening, I boarded my train back to NYC, somehow more enlightened than when I had arrived and totally smitten.

I arrived back at Jenny's flat in Queens that evening to find Daniel and Neleen sitting in the small garden leading to the front door. It felt as if I had walked in mid-argument, as I could have cut the atmosphere with a knife. After a brief conversation about my trip, Neleen went inside the flat, leaving just Daniel and myself. The weekend had not gone well for them; he had been proverbially flogging a dead horse insofar as Neleen was concerned, seeming she had lost interest way back in Tampa. We sat there talking for a few minutes whilst sharing a cigarette before proceeding inside the flat to join the girls. It wasn't long before a commotion had broken out in the kitchen; next thing, Neleen, car keys in hand, could be seen driving off. I never saw her again.

The next morning, the elephant in the room at breakfast was undoubtedly the lack of interest our advert had generated for our van. We had just over a week to leave the country; our funds had diminished to near dire straits, and we were running out of ideas. We did have one interested party who had made arrangements with Daniel whilst I had been in Boston. A corporate lawyer.

Two hours before the meeting, we set about preparing the van for a seamless viewing experience. The biggest issue we had was the transmission; it had never been right, however, after 15,000 miles, it was almost shot. The manifestation of this was it would often cut out whilst idling. We found the best antidote to mitigate the problem was a thirty-minute warmup. As we hadn't exactly been inundated with interest, we went all out with this opportunity.

A few minutes into the test drive, the guy, suspecting a transmission problem, asks permission to drive to a local transmission place to get a professional opinion. Our hearts sank as we reluctantly agreed; subsequently, we pulled into the first place we saw. Daniel and the lawyer got out and entered the premises, whilst I waited in the van. Ten minutes later, the two of them appeared and with a burly mechanic in tow. The mechanic plonked himself into the driver's seat, turned the key and took the van for a spin around the block. At this point, my mind was racing through options of how to fire sale the van to meet our visa exit expiration deadline. Once back, the mechanic hopped out of the van and exclaimed, "Chev, the best transmission in America." Van sold!

Later that evening, whilst out celebrating on the banks of the Hudson with a six pack, Daniel proudly explained how he had slipped the mechanic his last 50 bucks, whilst nobody was looking, to seal the deal. I had truly travelled with the master. We had just ripped off a New York lawyer. It felt awesome.

We had already received the deposit, and we were to rendezvous with the lawyer at his place of work in La Guardia in two days, precisely one day before our visa ran out, to close the deal. Then disaster struck. The van stopped working. Every morning with an almost near paternal attitude, we would religiously start the engine to warm it up, just to keep it going. That morning, the starter motor died.

One of the things I really came to appreciate about the United States was the deep sense of community spirit and self-organisation that seemed to prevail wherever we went. Our street in Queens was no exception. We had over the past two months become quite a feature of the area; word had spread about the two strange long-haired guys with the blue van. and by the end, we had made acquaintance with a good few of the characters that lived there, so much so that at one stage. it seemed the whole area had mobilised to help us with our plight of selling the van.

That morning was a testament to the community spirit prevalent in our area; word spread fast that our van had conked out, and within minutes, half the street had come to join us to push the van up the road to the local Turkish service place. After a morning of nervously explaining our predicament to the mechanic on duty, a long negotiation to get the job done ASAP for as little as possible and an agonising wait, we finally had our van back, complete with new starter motor; however, we were down to our last few dollars, very little fuel and about 40 hours to the proverbial bewitching hour.

The next morning, we packed our bags and said our goodbyes to Jenny; we were so gratuitous to this woman who had taken us in and made so much possible for us during the last few months. That day, we were going to deliver our van to its new owner, take the cash and purchase two tickets out of the country. Driving to Laguardia later that morning was as nerve-racking as it was exciting; we got lost twice and almost ran out of fuel in the process. Upon arrival at the bland office building in question, we approached the security desk and petitioned for the lawyer to come and meet us downstairs. Fifteen minutes later, we were on the subway on our way to Manhattan with 2500 dollars and the number plate in hand. Mission accomplished!

We had 16 hours to get out of the country; again, the research and contacts I had acquired way back in South Africa were going to pay dividends. Seemingly, I had jotted down an 1800 number for a very dynamic student travel agency based in Arizona. I decided to give it a try. I went to a payphone, punched in the numbers and requested two tickets out of the Tri-State area to anywhere in Europe that night. Minutes later, we were on the subway again to an affiliated student travel bureau at Columbia University, to pick up two tickets to London, ex Newark, which I had purchased, the last two seats on a Virgin Atlantic flight that evening.

Totally high on relief and success, we spent the better part of the afternoon pigging out on beer and ribs at a Sbarros near Madison Square Garden until it was time to board the airport bus to Newark. We had no idea what we were going to do when we got to London; we just knew that our two-man team that had stood the test of the American road trip had run its course. We were in the final chapter, and we both seemed to acknowledge the fact. What had started out as a chance meeting in Johannesburg four months ago had led to the most epic three months of my life I had come into myself so to speak. The lie instilled by upbringing, school and country had been decimated. I realised there was another way; there was no going back.

I did two things before I left the country that night: firstly, I put a call through to Kim in Boston to say goodbye, and secondly, I successfully flipped for the remaining number plate we had of the van. Up and till that point, I had, without fail, lost every coin toss played against Daniel. I saw this as symbolic that I had learned everything I needed from him and would be able to stand on my two feet now. Also, the number plate was the ultimate memento. I still have it till today.

Riding the Piccadilly line that morning after having left NYC the night before was akin to having boarded a bullet train and woken up in a steam train; the contrast those days between NYC and London in terms of freneticism couldn't have been starker. I had spent two months in London a few years before and had been somewhat overwhelmed; now, it felt like a village. That morning, the carriage was strewn with remnants of leftover newspapers headlining the Khobar Towers attack in Saudi, in which an office block housing US Airforce personnel was successfully targeted by a truck bomb, courtesy of Hezbollah. It was June 26, 1996.

After what seemed like a few hours, but actually much less, we found ourselves in a small park on a lovely London summer's day. Years before whilst travelling in Holland, Daniel had opened a Dutch Post Office Bank account and as a result, been issued with denominated cheques totalling a few thousand gulden. We had been sitting all of a few minutes when Daniel promptly got to his feet and proceeded to a UK post office outlet situated on the edge of the park, cheque book in hand to try his luck. Unbelievably, it worked; half an hour later, after what basically constituted daylight robbery, brimming with pride and a few thousand pounds richer after cashing his cheques, he returned.

He then stuck out his hand and wished me goodbye. To my surprise, he had decided to take a train to Manchester to rest up with his UK-based family for a couple of weeks before making his next move. He had enough money to fulfil his dream of going to India that summer. I was truly alone for the first time in my life with no plan.

The Dam

I just sat there as I watched his all too familiar shape walk into the distance and out of sight; a degree of panic set in. Up until now, all the time I had travelled alone had been time-boxed and very planned. After a while, I pulled myself together, donned my pack and intuitively started making my way to Earls Court, where I hoped to get a hostel for a few nights to figure out my next move. Those days, Earls Court was a hotspot for backpackers and independent travels alike. It wasn't too long after I stepped out of the tube station before punters from all walks of life were handing out commission-based accommodation vouchers. I knew one would be as bad as the other, so I randomly picked one. The flyer was innocuous enough; two things stood out, the map and the punter's signed name. Obviously, he needed to collect his commission. Without further ado, I walked the short distance to my chosen establishment and checked in.

I had picked a cheapie, as I needed to keep an eye on the cash flow situation. After the air ticket and a few sundries, my portion of cash from the sale of the van didn't look that healthy. I was assigned to a cramped unisex room, consisting of about 12 bunk beds. At the time I checked in, none of my roommates were around. I took the rest of the day to reacquaint myself with the city. As I had already spent a few months in London on a previous trip, I decided that I wanted to keep traveling. I was particularly interested in Eastern Europe and South America. The latter was not an option, as I didn't have the funds necessary for such a long-haul trip; thus, I spent the next few days putting together a basic plan of how I would execute a European trip. I spent my days squatting in bookshops, reading up on the different countries and the transport links that existed. In my evenings, I questioned fellow travellers that had done similar. After about two days, it was time to make a decision. I figured if I could sleep on the trains akin to how I had used the van for accommodation, then I could probably survive for about a month. I also realised that I needed to return to London after the trip and thus needed to make provision for surviving long enough before being able to secure work. After considering my options, I decided against the safe option of securing work and staying in London and impulsively bought a train/ferry ticket to Paris for the next morning. That evening, I shared a sandwich dinner with an American bloke in his late 40s I had met randomly in the hostel. I will never forget the advice he imparted to me that evening; he explained that whenever he was down to his last few dollars, his immediate reaction would be to spend it all. Always have an abundant mindset, he explained. Seemed totally counterintuitive, but somehow reassuring; if all went to plan, I would be arriving back in London in a month on the bones of my backside.

The next morning, I boarded my train for Dover. It was a bleak and overcast London that I was leaving behind. I had only spent a couple of days there but was happy to be on my way again. As the train chugged out of the station, all you saw was this grey molasses of an urban sprawl that seemed to capture within it 200 years of industrialisation, like a layered sentiment of sorts, old metal railway bridges from 150 years ago, locks, barges, concrete highways from the '60s, tenement houses from the '40s and modern office towers, all coexisting. The landscape eventually gave way to the countryside and little villages and remained that way until I reached Dover. In no time, I was on the ferry crossing the English Channel to France. At the bar on the ferry that morning, I was lucky enough to run into a young guy from the UK on his way to explore Paris for a few days. He had been there several times and thus I decided to join him for a day to get a taste of the city. My plan was to spend no more than one night in the city before heading up to Amsterdam. At Calais, we boarded a train to Gare du Nord and subsequently made our way to Père Lachaise, where we spent most of the afternoon getting high with a group of kids that we found sitting around Jim Morrison's grave. The rest of the day was a blur, jumping in and out of metros taking in the sites.

The next morning, after spending the night in a very clean, well-run hostel, I purchased a ticket to Amsterdam for that evening. At some point during the day, I spent a couple of hours in a fast-food outlet, writing a letter to Kim on the back of the paper tray cloth as I had no paper. I had only met her only two weeks prior, but Boston felt like a lifetime away. I never actually meant it to be a letter; it was more a therapeutic exercise than anything. In the letter, I tried to narrate my experience thus far and how I felt about my present situation; it felt more like a diary entry, diarising my feelings and thoughts was not something I had ever attempted before in my life. I seemed compelled to sit and write it, thinking back, probably to try and make sense of my decision and allay any fears I had. In the letter, I tried to explain how I had grown up in a culture of safety, where risks were to be avoided at all costs. The unknown was for others and only became viable when it transformed into the known. Paris felt extremely foreign and almost like a precursor to what lay ahead of me for the next couple of weeks; it would only become more foreign as I delved further and further into the unknown. The biggest psychological challenge was to battle my scarcity mindset that bedevilled me not only from nurture but from the real fact that I would be returning to London and not a safe harbour. Thus, I would need enough funds to set up there; every decision became an exercise in delayed gratification versus splurging. The finished letter read more like a personal insight. I franked the letter with the poste restante: Paris – as I had no idea where I would be if and when Kim ever decided to write back. However, I knew in a couple of weeks, I would be going back to London via Paris.

Amsterdam was going to be my last stop before the proverbial jump into the deep end; this, as I had a high school friend based there temporarily with his family for an extended holiday, who I was hoping to crash with. I had sent him an email that morning. Actually, he was the only person I knew who actually had an email. In 1996, there were only about 100,000 websites in the world. I shared my coupe that evening with a young American guy, spoiled and entitled, but friendly enough and we seemed to hit it off quite well. After having spent a few weeks with the extended family in Paris, he was on his way to Amsterdam before catching a flight back home. I was grateful for the company. I found the European types quite reserved and indifferent; this guy reminded me of my recent trip to the US. His plan was simple, check into a youth hostel he knew by recommendation and enjoy all the drug amenities on offer. By the time I boarded the train that evening, I still hadn't received a reply from my friend; however, I did have his family's landline number. I resigned myself to the fact I would call him from a local payphone once I arrived.

We arrived very early that morning in Amsterdam Central Station; little did I know then but this canalled city would later become my home for almost eight years. Amsterdam had a totally different atmosphere to Paris, and I much preferred it. Thinking I had a few hours to kill before the city actually awoke, I joined my new American friend on his pilgrimage to his hostel. After fiddling with a few maps, getting a little lost and ringing a menagerie of doorbells, we eventually found ourselves walking up the steepest staircase I had ever encountered. I spent the morning there chatting and smoking whatever was offered me till it was time to go. Ten minutes after leaving, stoned and tired, I could be found meandering around the canals looking for a payphone. At some point, I must have managed to find one and call because later that morning, we met up at a tram stop near VondelPark.

Ed was my closest friend I had had in high school; like me, born in South Africa to foreign parents, in his case Dutch, we had met in computer science class and became study partners. He himself was brilliant. I merely looked on in amazement with what he could do with software. I had only taken the class, as I was not interested in any other extra mural activities on offer; by my whites, only co-ed high school and thus had the time. In fact, like him I was not interested in being at the school at all. As a native English speaker growing up in predominantly Afrikaans area, the choice of high schools was limited to basically one. Government high schools were instruments of the apartheid state, their primary purpose to impart the party doctrine and prepare young men like myself to be cannon fodder in an ideological war we could neither afford nor win. They were the most miserable years of my life. I hated everything about it, the brown uniform, the kids, the teachers and the curriculum. The school like everything else in my life thrived on control; everything was measured, hair length, tie length, shoe polish – the list was endless. Every morning, we would line up for roll call like some sort of Nazi youth brigade. Mondays, we had the honour of an assembly which required us to stand and sing both the school and national anthems. The national anthem being a tribute to white supremacy and all it had achieved in Southern Africa. Corporal punishment was rife and almost encouraged; every time you broke the rules, you were summoned to the headmaster's office, given the privilege of choosing your cane from a selection, then told to assume the position until you felt the pain. The tradition those days was to record every hit on the back of your tie with a permanent marker akin to Baron von Richthofen recording a kill. Interestingly enough, the English curriculum had rather counter-intuitively introduced me to the structure of the dystopian construct I was growing up in, by lavishing me with literary works from the likes of George Orwell, Aldus Huxley, Rad Bradburg and many others. It was almost comical.

The next few days were a respite from the previous almost four months of travelling. For the first time since I had left South Africa, I had access to a proper bed. Even when we stayed with Jenny in Queens, we took turns sleeping on her couch or in the van; her small flat was way too small for all three of us. Life regained a semblance of normality during my time in Amsterdam and as such, I was really able to enjoy the city. By that stage, I had realised there was nothing romantic about travelling around the world on a shoestring; large swaths of time spent waiting punctured by bursts of energy to maximise limited opportunities, the afterglow the experience seemed to take on contrasted with the daily routine, I guess like most things in life.

For most of my time in Amsterdam, I was stoned or tipsy, and I couldn't think of a better way to explore that city. The easy-going laissez faire feeling seemed to permeate around the canals and narrow streets. I felt totally at ease in this pedestrianised village of a city. Amsterdam in 1996 was a very different place then it is today; even the trams were a different colour, an easy-going yellow, dotted with adverts as opposed to the strict blue uniformed pattern they carry today. This was of course years before the Pim fortuin and Theo van Gogh murders. Amsterdam would eventually become my de facto safe place in Europe, and about ten years later, I would quit my corporate job and long-term relationship to move there on a whim. My evenings were spent dotting in and out of small cafés, each packed to the ceiling with patrons and blaring loud music. Most of them were no bigger than a studio flat; however, when compared to the mega clubs in Florida, totally chic and authentic and far more enjoyable.

The afternoon I had planned to leave, I spent at a coffee shop with the cousin of my friend. It was in fact his family that I had been staying with. His plan was simple: get me stoned and put me on my train to Prague. I remember very little of that afternoon and the ensuing goodbye. All I know is

I made it aboard my train as I woke up three hours later in Cologne confused and panicked. I had just enough cognitive energy and time to navigate to my connecting train.

Time Travel

The next day, I woke up in Prague, hungover and deshelled from a night crawled up on a seat in a shared second-class coupe. As I walked out of the station, I had no idea where I was going; I just followed the majority of the crowd. Not long after disembarking, I found myself in the middle of the city. What I found was a quiet deserted place that seemed to be stuck in a different era. I had arrived as usual without any sort of plan. The only reference I had of Prague was the book by Milan Kundera, The Unbelievable Lightness of Being; however, at the time I read it, I was not sure I had had the life experience to actually understand it all. Still, notwithstanding my abridged understanding of the book, I at least understood something of the 1968 spring uprising and tried to use that as a reference with which to understand the city, which had only recently been freed from the scourges of communism. Having grown up in South Africa under a different type of dystopia, one that painted the Soviet Union with the same brush as Geroge Lucas' death star, I realised it was a poignant moment, as this was the first ex-communist country I had ever been to. Being branded as a communist in South Africa back in the '80s was worse than being accused of being homosexual. The understanding was that being born black was not a choice but a cruel affliction dealt by the hand of fate. Being born white and being either a communist or gay or worse, both, would be seen as a disease that needed intensive treatment to cure. Much like the concept explored in Arthur Miller's The Crucible, these terms would be used to sanitise and brandish individuals with a view to exerting control via self-censorship and spying. It's interesting as I write this that these exact same measures are themselves being used to great effectiveness by the world's contemporary left wing via social media and its culture of tagging, to the same end, in effect modern-day witch hunts.

I hadn't planned to spend very long in Prague and was anxious to keep moving; also to save money, I was going to spend as many nights as possible on the slow-moving night trains that were an almost permanent fixture on European railways those days. I spent most of the day in and around the astronomical clock. In 1996, it was the preserve of the backpackers and bohemian types, not unlike Washington Square Park in NYC. I found solace in these places, either engaging in conversation with like-minded individuals or simply alone reading a book whilst people watching. I was never one to tick tourist attractions off; that spreadsheet mentality is not something I could ever reconcile with. I was looking for an experience and atmosphere. For me, travel was about self-exploration and less about tourist attractions. I was looking for authenticity and in 1996, Eastern Europe offered a window into a different time. It was before all the big western shops had moved in lock stock and barrel; the people were still attached to their local traditions and unfazed by the lure of western trappings. However, even then I could see, that was changing fast.

That night, I boarded a train for Budapest. After being impressed with the little I had seen of Prague, I was keen to travel deeper into Eastern Europe. The train to Budapest was relatively empty compared to my previous journeys, and for this, I was grateful; however, I did have to share my coupe with two other travellers that night: an American couple of similar age to myself. The woman was confident, beautiful and thin, with a Mediterranean complexion and stunning black hair. The boyfriend by comparison was shy, conservative and corpulent. Both were wearing beige chino shorts and seemed to be dressed for a day at American University. Within no time, I had struck up a conversation with them and learned that she was of Romanian descent and was on her way to Bucharest to visit family for the summer; the plus one was just along for the ride. I quickly developed a rapport with both of them but specifically the girl. They were both reciprocally interested in me and my story. At that stage, I started to resemble a seasoned traveller and had the experiences to back it up. My long hair and unkempt look seemed to intrigue her as much as hers intrigued me. We chatted deep into the night, exploring the allure of the hidden danger that presented itself to each of us from one another. I frustratingly fell in love with her in minutes and couldn't bring myself to leave them in peace. It felt so strange to have a deeply personal conversation with and by implication form a connection with her in front of her plus one, who, by this stage, had fallen asleep. Just before arriving in Budapest, she wrote me her family's address and number and invited me to come and stay with them when I arrived in Bucharest, which was my planned next stop after spending a day or so in

Budapest. I gleefully accepted the contact details and bid them both farewell as I disembarked the train.

Walking around Budapest that morning with my backpack, my mind was still on the conversation from the previous night, and although I had not slept much, I felt very alive. After a short meander around the city, I purchased some food and headed for Buda Castle and its surrounding nature to enjoy a picnic lunch overlooking the Danube. To think I had been commuting on freeways to a drab business park for work on the outskirts of Johannesburg but only four months earlier was hard to comprehend and almost laughable. Thinking back to the day when Daniel's mum had persuaded me to follow my heart and not my upbringing brought a sense of personal satisfaction, although years before the movie, I would come to realise that on that day I had taken the red pill. The afternoon was spent in the famous Gellert baths a short distance away from the castle. In 1996, they were state-sponsored and cheap as chips; I got change for a dollar after spending over two hours there.

Budapest was an oasis on my trip. Again, I never got to see much; however, I had been bitten so much that I would over the course of the next 20 years visit over 30 times and even work there for short periods of time. That evening's plan was much the same as the day before, head to the train station later that evening in time to catch the slow train to Bucharest, where I was hoping to meet with the girl I had met the night before. Unlike the train to Budapest, this evening's train was packed and raucous enough to be considered a mobile party. I ended up bunched in with a group of loud young crazy Austrians that were on their way to Istanbul. I forget just how many characters made up the gang, but as usual, one caught my attention, and a very provocative girl that formed part of the group, Julia, reminded me of Kim a little, same short mousy brown hair and similar build, however, totally over the top and not shy of alcohol. She had wanted my attention since I had boarded, and it didn't take long for her to get it. That night I joined in with my newfound Austrian friends and drank and smoked until we collapsed. At one stage, it seemed most of the carriage had joined our coupe party. By the time we arrived in Bucharest, Julia had me around her little finger. I now had to make a choice; on the one hand, I wanted to continue the party that had started on the previous night's trip, and on the other, I wanted to meet the girl who I had met two nights before. I had about three hours before the train to Istanbul was scheduled to leave and decided to take some time out to think about it. I thought the best thing to do was to take a walk outside the station and get a feel for the city for an hour and see how I felt. I hadn't stepped but five metres out of the station when I was literally accosted by what seemed like tens of ravenous kids; they seemed to have their hands everywhere begging and taking what I had. One of the worst experiences I had to date on my trip. I knew something of the desperate history of the country, but I was not prepared for the horrific poverty that beset me that morning. I couldn't give them what little I had to give fast enough; it was like being attacked by a swarm of locusts. I later learned that they were most probably Roma kids, a term I had not heard previously. A group of people totally out of place with modern European society and treated as such. To say I had been blindsided by this incident would be an understatement, and thus with good consciousness, I decided to beat a retreat back to the station and re-join my Austrian friends, who, by this stage, had already secured all the alcohol needed for the 16-hour trip to Turkey via Bulgaria.

I never did see that Romanian American girl again; however, she did give me her email and as such, we kept in contact for about four years entertaining each other with stories of our subsequent adventures. We always promised to meet up if not on one of her modelling assignments in Italy then on one of my many return trips back to the US. Today, I see having had that small situation with the Roma kids knocked my confidence and subsequently caused me to leave Bucharest one of my biggest regrets on that trip. I lost focus. Coming from South Africa where I had seen abysmal poverty in relation to wealth, I shouldn't have dropped the ball.

A few hours later, I was held in with Julia and the rest of the Austrian gang, heading for Istanbul. It was going to be a long hot slog. What I had noticed since I left Amsterdam was that the quality of the trains and, thus by implication, level of comfort had progressively got worse with every train I took. It seemed that the further east and south I got, the worse it got, which made total sense of course as the countries I was travelling through since Germany had successively become poorer when compared to the previous. The trains were almost a metaphor for the country they traversed. The Dutch trains were clean but very modest, like the uniforms of the staff, which, like the oversized yellow tickets, gave me the impression I was in a theme park. The toilets would flush onto the railway tracks beneath with a sign above asking politely not to do this in the station; doing the right thing by society was the norm in Holland. The German trains were as clean, if not cleaner, but more luxurious. However, rules were enforced by the complement of conductors dressed in a more paramilitary-style uniform. Of course, the toilets flushed into a built-in septic tank. The trains in Czech and Hungary were quite similar in quality, second hand from Germany; most things were not serviced or were totally broken, and clean in parts. The conductors were more like secret police diligently checking your tickets for any sign of error; it was almost assumed you would be trying to short change the system. The coupes ranged from new to never having been renovated and seemed to represent a bygone age of 20 years before. By the time I found myself on the train bound for Istanbul, I could judge I had come a long way from Western Europe in a short time. They were ramshackle carriages at best, run by a mafia of conductors that seemed to treat the train and all within it as their personal fiefdom.

There was nothing to be seen out of the window; it seemed we were going through a very dry country. Inside, our spirits were high, as we kept the beer flowing and conversation raucous. However, it wasn't long before I noticed that Julia had started to lose interest. My novelty factor had begun to diminish in her eyes, and as such, I was slowly being side-lined. She was only 16; what did I expect? I had seen a similar type of attitude with Neleen with regards to Daniel back in the states. Notwithstanding this, I was getting along like a house on fire with the rest of the group and had decided to go with the flow and not take it personally – easier said than done – but what I couldn't manage to self soothe I outsourced to the beer and cigarettes. The advantage of having been accepted by a group had many advantages in the current situation; for one I was able to piggyback on their plans and research, which seemed to broadly fit into my strategy, and secondly I was less vulnerable to extreme situations, which, at this point in the journey, was invaluable. Of course, the social aspect was a boon as well.

Later in the day, we arrived at the border between Romania and Bulgaria. Standard procedure in 1996 was to stop allowing the respective country's immigration officers to stamp each and every passenger's passport. At this point in the trip, I had experienced this at every border crossing since leaving England without any issue. This was about to change. Everything started as expected. I readied my passport like I had done many times before and sat waiting for the Bulgarian immigration police to enter our coupe with their stamp. On entering, they were presented with five Austrian and one Irish passport. The Austrian passports were flipped through and stamped in minutes. My passport seemed to give them cause for concern; after flipping through it once to many by my count, and without the usual stamp, they disappeared for a while with my passport in hand. I remember this caused me some stress; it was the single most important document I had on me. I was also conscious I was on a train with little control of when it would leave again. After an agonising wait of what felt like way too long, the same police officer returned clearly irritated with two more officers. They all had the same puffed round faces with dark rings under their eyes, a most typical Bulgarian Duffy look. Without warning, they started shouting at me in broken English, something about the IRA and pointing to my long hair, whilst beckoning me to leave the train. I went cold; I had no idea where I was. Actually, I knew exactly where I was, in the middle of the small border town in one of the most corrupt places in Europe where nobody spoke proper English. Visibly nervous and by now sober from the morning drinking, I stood there next to the train facing these three immigration officials, who seemed convinced I was a terrorist. After a fruitless few minutes trying to negotiate with them and get a handle on the situation, my new Austrian friends dumped my backpack out the window and onto the floor at my feet and wished me luck, just as the train started making those typical train leaving sounds, whistling and screeching. My mind raced as I didn't want to end up there alone, then I remembered my friend Daniel and suddenly I knew what to do. Within five minutes, I was back on the train, twenty USD poorer, but resolute; it was a price worth paying to get out of the situation. The rest of the journey went without a hitch. However, something had changed. I realised just how vulnerable and alone I was in this world. I also realised I was able to problem solve in precarious situations. It was at that point I remembered something my mother had once told me before I left. She explained to me that money was my only friend; it was the only thing I would be able to count on in life. She was right. That advice stands true even today.

The 2nd border was crossed at 2 in the morning; albeit less stressful, it was as chaotic as could be. The Turkish border manned by soldiers seemed more fitting for a war zone. Again, as in the previous border crossing, money was doing the talking. Turkish visas were being issued on demand. However, for some reason, they were only accepting sterling; other hard currencies were being dissuaded by applying astronomical high exchange rates. It was beholden to each passenger to secure a visa, else there would be problems leaving the country in the future. It reminded me of those Ethiopian hunger scenes that would be flashed across our televisions in the late '80s whilst we sat eating our microwaved dinners in our suburban lounges. Crowds of desperate people running around UN uniformed personnel, who were dumping food from the back of trucks. Except in our case, it was the Turkish military dispensing visas surrounded by crowds of desperate people bartering for sterling from anyone who had. We were just missing Bob Geldoff and his Live Aid entourage.

Luckily, I was prepared, having my cash half in USD and half in Sterling. Unbelievably the chaos managed to sort itself out and we were soon on our way to our destination, Istanbul. The next morning, we rolled into town, it was quite simply the most exhausting leg of the trip thus far. It had been over two weeks since I had left London and three weeks since I had left NYC. That morning the culture shock hit me hard as we made our way through the ancient Ottoman city to the famous Bosphorus River where we boarded a ferry for the Arab side of the city. I was very grateful to be with the group now, even though they had already demonstrated their willingness to ditch me at the first sign of trouble. They had earmarked an area of two-star hotels where we would spend the next three days just relaxing. It might have been just a two-star hotel in the Arab section of the city, but on arrival, it left me with a feeling of absolute luxury compared to the shared coupes I had used as beds for the last week or so. My room was reminiscent of a jail cell, but at least it was mine and mine alone; shared bathrooms were the norm, but as we were the only guests, they seemed almost ensuite. The piste de resistance of the establishment was without a doubt the over-chlorinated pool complete with deck chairs and Unilever branded umbrellas. I felt like a star.

Sickness

For the next three days, I played tourist cum holidaymaker. I would while away my time at the pool, smoking and hanging out with the group. Other days, I would explore some of what the city had to offer. I was never much of a tourist, but I gave it a go in Istanbul. Unfortunately at this stage, my infatuation with Julia had grown whilst her interest had waned. This aspect started to weigh heavily on me and was a major reason for still keeping with the group. I had seen a similar pattern with Daniel and Neleen. The more I tried to get her attention, the less interested she became. The situation was going nowhere and had started to resemble a Tom and Jerry episode. She was a total minx and knew it and revelled in the thought of having me around her little finger. My emotional maturity and level of self-awareness were still in kindergarten, whilst my survival skill had graduated. What struck me about this group and others like them that I had met on the trip was the level of independence and maturity they exhumed. At 16 or 17 years of age, I would never be let go on a trip around the country on a train with a six pack of beers. The scourge of growing up with overprotective controlling parents and left an indelible mark on my psychological well-being. Not to mention the destructive influence of the Catholic church, which, at the end of the day, was used to unwrite almost every decision.

My parents, however, were as much victims as they were perpetrators. Fear and guilt were the mainstays in our house, and the apartheid regime took care of whatever free will and creativity that was left. It was in those weeks training it around Europe that I was introduced to the anecdotes of secularism and found it very appealing.

Three days later, we packed up and boarded a train for Athens. Having recuperated somewhat from my tirade of non-stop train journeys, I felt ready to carry on. It was an early departure and after boarding, I tried to get some sleep. A few hours later, subsequent to having passed the Greek border, a total disaster struck, one the girls in the group fell violently ill. Nothing we did for her helped and the more time that passed the worse she got, to the point where she became quite delirious and disorientated. Dehydration was also becoming a concern as she had been vomiting a lot and we were unable to get her to consume any liquids. Trying to get any help from the conductors or train officials was like pulling hen's teeth; people were either indifferent or incompetent or both. It was at this stage that we made the difficult decision to pull her off the train at the next station. As soon as the train came to a stop, the Austrians went from drunken louts to a group of boy scouts; with almost military precision, she was stretched off, placed in a taxi and rushed to the nearest hospital. I was sitting there on the platform with the remainder of the group that remained a while later as the train pulled felt totally surreal. We spent a good hour there waiting to get word from the girls who had rushed off to the hospital; eventually, our boredom and our anxiety got the better of us, and we pooled the funds to order our taxi of our own to the hospital. It was a small town of no more than about 10,000 people, which we figured would not have warranted more than one hospital. After a hell ride in an old 1979 Mercedes Benz taxi, we ended up on the outskirts of town at the doors of the hospital. Walking in conjured up images of what I had read about in books about the Crimean war. The place was filled to the brim with sick people, and there was a flurry of doctors everywhere. It was a struggle to figure out where to go as nobody really spoke English; however, nobody stopped us walking around. Eventually, we got sight of her surrounded by the other half of the group. She was wired up to machines and drips. Food poisoning had done this, we presumed something she had eaten that morning in Istanbul. Luckily, they had all had the presence of mind to take out private health insurance. Her trip was over; she was taken by ambulance to the local airport later that day and flown back to Vienna before nightfall. She was back in the part of Europe that worked. The rest of us bussed it back to the railway station that evening and waited for a train to take us to Athens.

By now, I was an almost permanent member of the group, and we had become good friends over the last week or so. They seemed to really appreciate that I tried to help in the emergency situation that had transpired. I had been quite key in insisting we get off the train and to a hospital soonest. It's a well-known fact within my closest circle of friends that I can be quite neurotic at times; this time, I like to think it saved somebody's life. We later heard she had to spend two days in hospital but eventually made a full recovery.

We quickly set about finding accommodation; we only planned to stay one night, long enough to take in a few key tourist sights. We ended up securing an overpriced hostel with space for us on the roof. It was high season, and the city was brimming with backpackers and interrailers alike. Athens seemed more like a dust bowl than democracy. Our mood was rather more sanguine than normal due to the emergency that had transpired the day before. I could see the group had largely given up on the trip and were mentally preparing to go back home. I of course had no such plan; actually, at that stage, I had no idea where home was anymore. It certainly wasn't South Africa; I had changed too much. In my mind, as I was to return to London after the trip, that was going to be my adopted home albeit I knew nobody there. The next few days were spent getting to Italy via trains and a night ferry.

At Brindisi on the Italian coast, I, with a heavy heart, bid farewell to Julia and the gang that I had spent two weeks travelling with. I had failed to keep her attention, and our journey together had now finally run its course. After swapping numbers and addresses, they boarded their train and departed. I spent the rest of the day taking in the scenery whilst trying to acclimatise to being alone again. The next few weeks took me from Venice to Vienna, then on to Hamburg and finally onto Stockholm with a day stopover in Copenhagen. By the time I reached Stockholm, my health and my cash had been spent. I disembarked that morning feeling like I needed to visit a hospital. My health insurance had long since expired after I had left NYC. Psychologically, I was at my end. I had wanted to go to the Arctic Circle, but as I crawled into the overpriced toilet cubicle in Stockholm station that morning, and rolled my sleeping bag on the floor, the only thing I could think of now was surviving long enough to make it back to Amsterdam, where I could hopefully crash with my friend again. I decided to camp in the toilet cubicle as my stomach was liquid and my temperature sky high. The next 24 hours took an incredible amount of mental strength just to make it through. I kept thinking of that girl in Greece who had ended up in the hospital and forced myself to drink water; it was about the only thing I could keep down, just. Problem-solving became very difficult, working out times and schedules and exchange rates became incredibly complex to manage. That evening after a dire eight hours spent in the cubicle fighting off the cleaners and I think the security even made an appearance at one point, I can't be sure, I managed against all odds to put myself onto the next train back to Copenhagen. I literally slept in a pool of sweat sitting up on the seat that night, forcing water down every time I could. When you are sick, the world does not want to know you. The next morning, my fever had still not broken, and my head felt like it was wrapped in a vice, and I had not eaten much in almost 48 hours. Luckily, I didn't have long to wait for my connection, as I decided to take the fast train back and take the financial hit. By the time I reached Amsterdam, I had actually started to feel better and was able to navigate to my friend's family's house with relative ease. In the next two days, I divided my time between sitting in the bath and sleeping in bed. I was so grateful for that opportunity, I am not sure I would have had the strength to make the journey to London in that precarious state, also my funds had been exhausted. I was down to my last hundred pounds sterling. I was looking at arriving in London with enough resources to last about a week. Amsterdam served as an oasis for me again and gave me the time to heal my body whilst mentally preparing for the next stage of my trip, moving back to London, broke.

Why London? I had thus far seen many more beautiful cities on my journey than London, each with their own specific charms; however, when it came to the task at hand, none were fit for purpose. I needed a city that demanded workers without the red tape, a dynamic place where decisions were made in minutes, not weeks or months. I needed access to housing without being bothered with all the rules that were supposed to protect tenants. I was not interested in rights. I needed a city that spoke English that was set up to deal with a revolving door of Antipodeans, Irish and South Africans alike, a city that knew the language of winging-it, a city connected to every corner of the world. It was the only city in Europe I could think of those days that would accept a stranger with a goal who was willing to do almost anything to achieve. A most ruthless place.

London

It wasn't long before I felt back to my normal self and was able to make the short trip back to London via Paris and across the English Channel. During my layover in Paris, I took the time to visit the main Paris post office in the vain hope I might have a letter waiting for me from Kim. Alas, I left empty handed; however, not before penning another one to her with a brief description of my recent whirlwind trip around Europe. This time, I gave no return address, only a promise to write again soon when I had managed to settle a little in London.

I arrived early in the evening and made my way directly to the youth hostel I had stayed in before for no other reason than it was familiar and cheap. That night trying to settle in, I met some of the crazy people I was sharing a room with. They all seemed to be friends and as such, I felt a little estranged; after a brief introduction, I turned in for the night. The next morning, after being served a bowl of Kellogg's Rice Krispies and powdered milk, the only breakfast on offer, I was offered some work in return for a free night by the owner. Not having anything in particular to do, I took the opportunity. Seemingly, the place was visited by inspectors every month to check whether they were adhering to their fire safety regulations. Each hostel was in fact licensed to only have a certain number of beds. My job was to help disassemble five beds and hide them before the inspectors were to arrive later that afternoon and then help resemble them once they had left. To this day, I never did figure out if they were tipped off on the impending inspector visits or if they had to have announced themselves beforehand by law. All in all, I was happy to assist and dutifully helped break the law that day.

I spent most of the rest of the day talking to fellow travellers about their respective journeys thus far. The next day after the same disgusting breakfast, I was offered more work in return for a payment in kind. The task was simple: go out and entice ignorant and willing backpackers just off the boat to stay in the hostel. In return, based on a threshold, I would be offered a few nights for free. The drill was simple, walk about a mile to Earl's Court tube station and wait just outside the entrance, with a few brochures with my name inked on them, profile for ignorant backpackers and approach with all my charm. Initially, I was met with relative success and managed to do well; however, it was very time consuming and the constant rejection eventually left me burnt out. When I wasn't canvassing for backpackers, I was doing manual work for one of the many manual outsourcing bureaus that existed. This required getting up early in the morning, walking about three miles to the agency's office to see what was on offer. I was either told there was nothing for the day or bundled in the back of a panel van and driven to the outskirts of the city, to work in some or other distribution centre. These jobs almost without fail required either packing or sorting or both and were always paid on performance never per hour. Even though the work was mind-numbing, I was grateful for the opportunity. The highlights were always the coffee and cigarette breaks where I would engage with my fellow workers. I met so many people from so many walks of life, single mothers, breadwinners, backpackers, old, young, sick and healthy. We were all scraping the barrel at that point in our lives. It was the stuff of minimum wage and the working poor. A day's work if you were lucky would net you about 20 pounds, depending on your performance. On the days the agency had no opportunities, I carried on with my informal recruitment work for the hostel. One day, I decided to try my luck at Victoria Station, which I was told was not without risks, as unlike standing on the pavement, you were inside a Transport for the London building. It ended as fast as it started; I was detained by police, given a dressing down and sent on my way with a warning never to return.

In the initial days of trying to get on my feet, the two greatest impediments to getting out of the poverty trap so to speak were cheap long-term rent and stable work within walking distance of home. Luckily, I was soon going to be presented with an opportunity that would solve the accommodation issue. My hostel roommates had hatched a daring plan to rent a house long term. Most of them had been living in that hostel room for months and, like me, saw it as a money pit. The plan, the brainchild of an Asian Australian, Kate, revolved around her and another Australian guy sharing the room to pose as a respectable couple with a view to renting the two-bedroom house in question. Once agreed, the rest of the group would ditch the hostel and move in. Nine people in total. A complete nightmare situation with respect to the landlord. The plan also hinged on the fact the landlord lived in Wales and was rarely around to keep an eye on things. By the time I had arrived, the plan had been in motion for weeks.

However, rather surreptitiously, at the last minute, a Polish girl that had been earmarked as the ninth person to co-habit had cancelled. Seeing the opportunity, I pounced and was able to negotiate myself as the replacement, no mean feat considering the group had been living together as a pseudo-family in the hostel for over three months. I had not yet been there a week. Moving day was three days away, and I needed to raise a deposit and a month's rent. The work I had done for the labour broker was yet to be paid, and the work I had done for the hostel was paid in kind. I did the only thing I could and drained my credit card to its limit.

At this point, I was on the bones of my backside and had to consume tins of cheap canned food for nourishment. I was also having to rely on drawing cash from my foreign credit card with all the interest, withdrawal and exchange rate charges that went with it, just to cover expenses; for this, my agency jobs only paid fortnightly. I had always been conscious to keep contact with parents in order to pacify their fear of me ruining my life or ending up in some evangelical religious cult handing out Jesus pamphlets on the side of the road. To that, I had resigned myself to calling them at least once every four weeks. I remember once such a call during my initial days in London when they were less than happy to hear from me, due to the fact they had seen fit to open my bank statements for whatever reason and were decidedly irritated with what they found. I remember being equally irritated by having my post opened without my sanction. This was the typical relationship I had with my parents; there had not been very clear boundaries with anything. However dire my financial situation was at this stage, there was a plan. A couple of years before my grandparents had left me a small inheritance in Ireland, enough to cover setup costs in London, the problem I had was access to those funds, and thus I had decided to use my credit card facility as a proxy. This explanation did little to satisfy my rather irate parents on the other side of the world. What made matters worse was that they had already phoned the bank in a vain attempt to report my card was stolen, which would have paralysed me financially; lucky the bank had advised against it. There was no love lost in our relationship; this was especially true with regards to my relationship with my dad. If the situation had been tenuous before, the credit card statement detailing transactions in places far and wide only served to push it to near breaking point. That call would be my last for a while.

A few days later, nine of us checked out of the hostel and walked the short two miles to our new home in Shepherds Bush. The house was a classic two-story semi-detached complete with a small garden. Each of the rooms would be shared, except the oversized walk-in closet that would be used by Kate exclusively; her prize, if you wish, for coming up with the idea and executing it successfully. Compared to the cramped conditions in which we lived before, our new living conditions were a total luxury. The one downside was we had to share one bathroom between us. This move had come as a complete boon to me, especially considering I was able to escape the hostel within the first two weeks of having moved to London. All I needed now was a steady job close to home.

Luke and Keith, two crazy South Africans, moved into the dining room. They also seemed to be the gatekeepers of the bong and most of the other drug paraphernalia that came to inhabit the house. Luke, the resident drug alchemist, sported long hair like me and seemed to always wear black. He was tall, scrawny, slow speaking and mostly stoned; when he wasn't getting high, he was generally out doing hard labour jobs for minimum wage: demolition and construction type gigs. Keith was the house sociopath. I had run into the type a lot in South Africa; they reel in you with love bombing and a twist of emotional blackmail, then after a while, when you suspect things are not quite what they seem, they gaslight you. I will never forget his eyes; they seemed to stare into your soul. Despite his easy-going attitude and near-always high state, he never forgot anything you ever said. He was also the oldest in his late twenties and had the best paying job, working as a chef in a glamorous Covent Garden establishment. They both boasted British passports, but unlike Luke, Keith was from a wealthy middle-class family from Johannesburg Northern suburbs. Luke was a soutpiel from Vereeniging. The front room was shared by a couple from New Zealand. They were as interesting as cardboard cutouts; they both worked in the same pub, both wore the same type of clothes and seemed to live their own lives. They seemed to live the most vanilla lifestyle of all the housemates, only occasionally joining in with the rest of us. I never once heard them say anything interesting about anything. The only remarkable memory I have of the guy was his wallet, which always was attached to his oversized jeans by a chain. Somehow, this irked me. The other two South Africans who had coveted the biggest bedroom upstairs were two Afrikaners from the Free State, known to me as tweedle dumb and tweedle dumber; they seemed to share everything, including a brain. Life-long friends, they had decided to explore what lay beyond the safety of the Free State as a team. Friendly enough and helpful, but after four months in London, total drug addicts.

They both worked shifts at a local karting establishment, DayTona, as marshals; they also shared an annoying habit of using the diminutive form of nouns. For that reason, I kept conversation to a minimum. They were totally inseparable, and like a married couple, no decision could be made without the other's involvement. I shared the second bedroom with the Asian Australian guy from Perth. He seemed to have the right idea. He was in London for an experience, not a working experience per se; luckily, his parents bankrolled him. He spent his days in and around trendy markets and stores gathering music trinkets and interesting items of clothing. He also seemed to have an obsession with Jamiroquai, which only grew worse as time went on. I nicknamed him Jamiroquai-esque. We secretly hated each other. Kate from Melbourne oozed sex appeal, and by my account, she was the smartest of the gang I had met in that hostel. She had a 9–5 job working for British Telecom in a call centre and an affinity for ecstasy. Notwithstanding her charm and brains, she also seemed to have access to a whole string of equally beautifully charming Australian girls she had met at work. Insofar as I was concerned, their visits to the house were a respite to usual suspects that would use the house as a chill-out zone; these normally included the owners of the hostel we had just left and a few other strays that were still living there.

Those first days at the house were spent settling in and organising ourselves into a workable routine. Bathroom roasters were the biggest points of contention. I learned in those days that any democracy stops at the shared bathroom door. The second point of contention was the fridge and storage space and who had access to which shelf. This wasn't my first house share in my life, so I knew the drill; the rules were simple: you keep the bare minimum in the kitchen and everything else in your room. This was to protect against the milk and bread thieves that seemed to be a quintessential part of those setups. Getting a BT landline was also a big priority in the early days; landlines were cheaper and far more convenient than payphones. In 1996, the BT callbox was as indispensable as toilet paper to the backpacking community. All communication with home, work, insurance companies and airlines was done via the phone; not being able to receive calls meant getting hold of the right person or waiting for a call back. This often meant spending hours waiting in and around a payphone. I remember that during those early days, I would often set up a makeshift office in the phone box at the top of our street, spending about two hours there some mornings trying to organise work, etc. Mobile phones were still the preserve of the business class and the world wide web was very much in its infancy, especially in the UK. Smartphones were science fiction at that stage, Apple was almost bankrupt. It would be another ten years before the iPhone. It took Keith close to three weeks and multiple attempts from BT before we had the phone installed. Being the sociopath that he was, he would often use access to the phone as a form of conditioning when it situated him; any disagreement would be met with a jest threat of the phone privileges being removed. Living in that house almost became like living in a social experiment. The politics, backstabbing and entitlement on display by the various housemates, myself included, was akin to watching an episode of The Real World, the MTV reality TV show that was the precursor to the Big Brother franchise. My plan was simple: use it as a cheap base to enable me to save as much as I needed to travel to South

America. It was the end of July, and I was hoping to be out by the middle of October.

Not long after having moved in, I, at the suggestion of one the tweedle dumbs, decided to apply for a job at the karting establishment; seemingly, they were always looking for staff, and albeit a minimum wage job, it had the unique advantage of being walking distance from the house. The savings on transport and time were a distinct drawcard. The application process was simple: attend an informal interview and work two training sessions for free. If they liked you and you could follow simple orders and learn quickly, you were hired. Two days later, I was hired. Two weeks after moving to London, I had secured cheap housing and a regular job that would allow me to save, no small achievement considering London had a reputation those days for sucking in backpackers, enslaving them to hand to mouth existence and then spitting them out when they eventually couldn't take it anymore.

Routine

Life quickly became a routing of tiring shift work ranging from 4 in the afternoon to 2 in the morning. Schedules were planned weekly, and you took what you were given or you were out. The bosses were a mean lot, two obnoxious brothers who had inherited their money and invested it into two karting businesses. The organisation ran on fear. Profanities and expletives were the norm, and mistakes were not tolerated. It was the most toxic work environment I had come across in my short working life. The job revolved around standing at a nominated point on the track, dressing in a fireproof suit, sporting a flag and using a two-way radio for communications to the control tower and other marshals. Flags were used to communicate to the drivers to either slow down, speed up or stop based on the situation on the track, and you were expected to perform without hesitation in front of moving machines when required to pull karts out of the tire walls. It was dangerous and physical work; it was also done inside a warehouse building. Thus, the combination of never seeing the sun and the constant indigestion of carbon monoxide took its toll on your psychology and physical state. The job did, however, have a glamorous side, the races were done as a show, with fully choreographed light and music aspects that emanated a Grand Prix setting, complete with podiums and fake champagne. The clients were primarily corporates using it for team building events, tourists, famous actors and aspiring boy bands. My most notable tire wall rescue being that of one the members of the Backstreet Boys, which, at that stage, were just starting out and by no means famous. I met many such aspiring bands whilst doing that job, most never made it big. The Hollywood actors would book the redeye shift. This would start at 10 and end at 2; most of them would be high on some narcotics, and almost none of them ever took note of the rules. The highlight for me was helping some of the most desirable women in the world fit their helmets whilst sharing a joke. Once the proverbial fat lady had sung on the redeye shift, it took a further hour to clean up and pack up. For the privilege of working the redeye shifts, you were paid an extra pound an hour. Notwithstanding the fact I was not entitled to payment for the clean-up or preparation time, I was gratuitous for the consistency of the work as opposed to the ad hoc shifts that were available from the labour brokers. Work was, however, work, and on my days off from being a marshal, I was always keen to pick up a shift from the labour brokers if I could. My waking hours were consumed with working; most times, I would return home late only to find a party or drunken gathering of some sort. Sometimes I would even find strange people high in my room or even on my bed; none of this bothered me. I was simply to focussed and exhausted to care. Sleep came easy those days; mornings were more difficult. Dragging myself out the house for consecutive shifts became progressively more challenging as the weeks went by.

On those evenings, when I found myself without shifts, I would sometimes join whoever was in the house in whatever debauched activities they were engaged in. More often than not, this would involve sitting in Keith's and Luke's room listening to music and smoking a bong. Their room was the de facto gathering place, not surprisingly perhaps, as it had been designed as the dining room and by implication was connected to the kitchen. In all my time living in that house, I never once noticed a bed or mattress in that room; seemingly, they just slept on the floor. The house had become notorious in the local hostelling circles as the go-to place for drugs and partying, a legacy in part due to the roots of the inhabitants. More often than not, the house would be visited by friends and acquaintances made in those days before the move. Also, after a few weeks, the Polish girl who had abdicated as being part of the household originally due to financial problems had by now subsequently moved in as a permanent non-rent-paying resident. There had been an agreement in the early days to let her stay until she found her feet; somehow, the group had a soft spot for her, and I being very much an outsider I decided not to argue. What annoyed me the most was the fact that the household had decided her squatting place would be the floor space in my room. It didn't make much sense, as it wasn't even the biggest room. The room consisted of two beds, one for myself and the other for Jamiroquai-esque; she slept on the floor at the foot of my bed. In fairness, she paid the rent in her own way by being the maid and by connecting the household to her drug dealers. This woman was a walking disaster; she had no right to work in the country and seemed to be abused by any and every employer that hired her under the table. The story was always the same:

after a few days or shifts at a pub or restaurant, she would be fired without pay, and being illegal, she had no recourse except to call the Polish mafia to aid her. This inadvertently led to a couple of heavies going around to the establishment in question with a baseball bat to dispense mob justice. Mostly this worked, and she ended up getting her pittance. I remember one such incident when after having worked in a local Irish pub for almost two weeks, she again was thrown to the curb without pay. I truly felt sorry for her and was happy to see the Polish mafia at the house the next evening reading themselves to pay the miscreant paddy in question a visit. Not having much privacy in the house, I would often fall asleep to her having sex with either Luke or some German guy that everybody knew from the hostel. I never quite understood what she saw in either of them, but then, it was mostly drug-induced. Living in those conditions was a real test of my sanity. Seemingly obvious to all and sundry my other roommate, Jamiroquai-esque's endless tirades of trinket collection seemed to run at a tangent to the struggles being experienced by the rest of the household. I often thought he chose to stay with us to fulfil some voyeurism fetish because I am sure he could have afforded better. Tuesdays somehow turned into club nights, albeit at least for some of us. Mostly, I was working during this time; however, one Tuesday evening, I found myself at a loose end and allowed myself to be convinced by Kate to join her. As with most things that happened in that house club nights, came with a twist; it was not your usual going out to dance evening but an ecstasy-infused experience of which the club was just a conduit. The drill was always the same: some of the household would get a taxi to a club in Charing Cross at about 11:00, queue up and

119

pay to enter. On entering, they would 'case the joint' for whatever dealer was working the floor that evening. Eventually, a deal would be done and soon the group would be in another taxi homeward bound with a bag of ecstasy. That Tuesday was no different except for the fact I was part of the entourage that evening. I had never taken it before; the only thing I remember was sitting with Kate on her bed as she slipped a pill into my mouth. The rest of the evening turned into a love-filled ecstasy like no other I have ever experienced; that was the first and last time I tried that drug.

During my time there, the house also hosted numerous other visitors from lands afar. One character in particular that seemed to arrive almost without announcement was Keith's brother. He, for some reason, had undertaken a trip from South Africa and took it upon himself to bed down in our dining room. There never seemed to be a good explanation as to why he had come to London; then again, my experience of sociopaths' communication styles had always left me questioning everything I had been told. Getting either Keith or his brother to commit to a 'Yes' or 'No' answer was akin to nailing jelly to a wall. I got the feeling all was not well in Johannesburg, and the mother had seen fit to explore the option of moving the family's residence to the UK. Seemingly, having both sons on the ground so to speak would serve as a balanced reconnaissance mission before any decision was made. Both had the same beady eyes and were built like beef stroganoff, lanky and thin. The longer I stayed at that house, the more apparent it became I should leave. Discussions with those two characters almost always left me hanging and feeling uneasy. At some point, the fact that we had a phone played into its own when one evening members of a heavy metal band touring from South Africa, which had been crashing in a nearby basement, knocked on our door and asked if they might use our phone to receive a call from a famous South African DJ live on radio for an interview later that evening. Without thinking it was agreed, it was with almost comical theatrics when later that evening, three lanky blokes from Johannesburg waltzed into our house all with an air of self-importance reserved for only the most prominent of international stars and gathered around our phone like school girls waiting to prank call somebody. Seemingly, they had been relatively successful in the local alternative club scene back in South Africa and had, by hook or crook, ended up with a few gigs at a local London dive. Not having much of a budget, they had elected to stay in squalor near us. I still, to this day, don't recall how they heard about us and our phone facility. The interview went well insofar as we could hear; I was imagining the listeners back home hearing this on the respective late night show that I myself had diligently listened to back in the day, thinking how successfully and awe spring these primadonnas were. Whereas in reality, a rather different story was actually playing out on the ground.

Life became a sequence of struggles, and the time and energy I devoted to working and the delayed gratification I was enduring seemed disproportional to the gains being made. The longer I spent in that house with those characters, the more I hated it, and, by implication, the less tolerant I became. The work itself was also taking its toll on my physical health; notwithstanding the physical energy needed to enact the activity, I had come close to a few accidents. Moreover, I had seen a few of my colleagues stretched out with injuries never to return again. In the back of my mind, it felt like I had somewhat succumbed to my lot a bit. I remembered that a few months ago, when in the USA, my attitude had been very much can do when things got hard, here, in London, I felt as if I was in some sort of sinking sand. Everyone I seemed to meet seemed to be in a type of molasses; for the most part, they didn't even realise it. Unlike me, most had been seduced by the sex appeal and glamourous life the city purported to offer. I had always had a healthy contempt for the place, and after spending a good few months traveling around the USA, I could really see it for what it was in 1996, an oversized village on an island. Sure, it had its glamorous parts, but most cities did. I needed to get out and fast.

Reunion

Two chance meetings in quick succession were going to help propel me out of my funk in no time. Not long after my realisation with regards to my despairing situation, I received word that my father would be making a trip to Dublin to see family and had offered, albeit rather reluctantly, to meet me at Heathrow Airport whilst waiting for his connection. I agreed. On the day of our meeting, I dressed for work, as I needed to do a shift on my return and made the almost two-hour journey to the airport. Waiting anxiously at the airport for my father to walk out the arrivals hall, I couldn't stop thinking about the last time we had seen each other; it had only been about seven months ago, just before I caught my greyhound bus up to Johannesburg. We had been like two ships in the night during the days before I left, both stubborn in the righteousness of their own convictions. I had no idea what he was expecting to see when he walked out, but his eyes said it all. I must have been quite a sight, dressed in a fireproof Sparco suit, gunt, bruised hands and smelling of petrol. Our meeting lasted but ten minutes, and after giving me a letter from my mother, we shook hands, and he left with a seemingly newfound respect for his oldest son. His absolute shock at my state, however, served as a confirmation of just how bad my situation had become. A few days later, whilst enjoying a day off, I exited Earls Court tube station and, by chance, happened upon a conversation that took place within earshot of where I had been standing. The conversation centred around a larger-than-life individual from South Africa, seemingly ruthless but charming. After eavesdropping for a few minutes, I became intrigued and rather uncharacteristically interrupted the conversation and petitioned them about this individual on the premise I thought I knew the person. About ten minutes later, I walked into a two-star backpacking hotel and came face to face with Daniel. I was almost certain it was him I had overheard the punters on the street talking about. There had been no contact between us since that day he had hightailed it to Manchester. We just stood looking at each other in disbelief and in between nervous laughter, we pieced together our respective stories over the past two and half months. Daniel hadn't wasted any time up in Manchester and, not having been bound by a lack of cash, had decided to postpone India and instead had flown to Moscow and embarked on a journey across the country to Vladivostok on the trans-Siberian express, eventually ending up in Tokyo where he had remained until his money ran out. He had returned to London only a few weeks after I had for exactly the same reason: to replenish cash flow and embark on the next adventure. I hadn't felt this inspired since I met him that day in Johannesburg; the more he detailed his experiences of the last months, the more energised I became. Being almost pseudo brothers at this stage, he wasn't liberal with the details, and it soon became apparent that his next trip, to India, was almost financed, and his leaving was imminent in weeks not in months. Like everything with Daniel, there was a shortcut. In the USA, it was stolen credit cards before in London, it was cheque fraud. This time, it was medical tests. Unbeknown to me at that stage, London was an epicentre for organised drug trials for the large pharma companies. They were well paid and tax-free; you could make a month's wages in a week. Daniel had managed to do three simultaneously, totally illegal but very lucrative. The rest of the afternoon he carefully laid out step by step what I needed to do to reproduce his formula for success. I made sure to take meticulous notes. I left our meeting that day, feeling like I had ingested a bag of cocaine. I wouldn't see him again for many years, but I had a map out of London in my pocket, and for the first time in weeks, I could see an end to my London rut.

The next day, armed with my new-found knowledge, I registered my details with a local hospital providing organised drug trials. The registration procedure consisted of a call to voice machine where you were required to leave your contact details. A few days later, I received a call back concerning a stage-3 drug trial testing for a drug to treat haemophilia. After answering a few questions about smoking, drinking and any pre-existing conditions, I was asked to attend an intake interview. The best thing about those trials was that everything was paid not just the days in hospital but all visitations including the initial intake. The intake took place at the hospital a few days later; here, I was asked a few more basic health questions in the presence of a doctor and a representative of the pharmaceutical company and then presented an indemnity form to sign. It was clear that nobody was taking any chances; all risks were to be borne by me. The trial was to last six days during which time I would be admitted to hospital and have the drug administered under a

24-hour supervision whilst being monitored for any side effects.

To say it was a surreal experience walking into Guy's hospital a week later for my trial would be to downplay just how lost and detached I felt from myself. Somehow, my preoccupation with travel and getting out of London had become an obsession to the point where every thought and action had become a manifestation of the ruthless pursuit of my goals. I felt dead inside; all I could think of was the discussion I had with Daniel a few days before and how motivated I was to compete. I knew by the time I walked in there; I was prepared to do whatever it took to achieve my goals, however misplaced and toxic they had become. I totally discounted the possibility of any long-term effects; this was potentially going to have on my health and stupidity made my decision based on short-term gain.

That evening, on admission, I was assigned a bed in a ward with six other lab rats, all of us there to participate in the same drug trial. The evening consisted of signing more forms and having our vitals checked. Out of the six of us, one would be secretly given a placebo to be used as the control person for the cohort. Apparently, this was standard procedure in the business; frustratingly enough, nobody including the nurses running the trail was privy to that information. That evening after a sumptuous dinner, one of the best meals I had had since arriving in London, they turned the lights out. Surprisingly, sleep came easy that night; the orderly hum of the hospital machines almost soothing compared to the chaos that I would have ordinarily been subjected to back home.

The next morning, we were woken up early by a flurry of hospital activity and subjected to further checks ranging from blood pressure, sugar to an ECG. Sadly, the bloke lying next to me failed his ECG test that morning and was subsequently removed from the trial with a referral to a cardiologist. The doctor on duty had picked up an irregular rhyme, and due to the severity of the business at hand, specifically having healthy people to generate the most accurate results, he had been discharged. Notably worried, he scurried out like a piece dejected vermin, referral in hand. Things moved rapidly after that; each of us had two catheters inserted into each of our arms. Our left arms were subsequently wired up to a drug administrative machine, which somehow reminded me of the scenes I had seen in movies about death row inmates being executed. The catheter in the right arm was to be used to draw blood throughout the day and night. The nurses were very kind and professional as they went about sticking needles into us; thinking back on it, that is the only thing I have favourable memories of that day. Then at 7:00 am sharp, our machines were all loaded with five large syringes of the experimental drug and turned on. For the next two hours, a vial viscous liquid was injected into my arm at a snail's pace; moreover, the nurses would be engaged in activities ranging from taking blood, swabbing our mouths and checking our vitals. I don't recall how much blood they took, but it was a lot every half an hour for the morning, then it decreased to every other hour until eventually, it plateaued out at twice a day for the duration of the trial. Throughout the experience, I don't remember experiencing any side effects from the poison I had subjected my body to. I kept myself sane by chatting to the nurses and my fellow lab rats. They were from different walks of life, all with different reasons for needing the cash; the most interesting story was from a guy who had a job as a teacher and often used this as a way to supplement his income during school holidays. Like Daniel, he had explained to me the best trials were those that had been tested on people before, as for the most part any negative effects would have already played out.

Just before the drug trial, I paid a visit to a local second-hand bookstore to purchase some reading material to pass the time whilst in hospital. They had made mention before the trial that for most of the time we would not be bedridden and would have access to a lounge area with satellite TV, a big thing in 1996. I had never been one for television, and my experience in the USA of just how dumbing it could be had done little to change my mind. I had always been an avid reader of George Orwell and was pleasantly surprised to find a copy of his first full-length novel Down and Out in Paris and London on one of the shelves. I couldn't think of a more apt book at that time in my life. I was not wrong; in my mind's eye, I had sunk to the lowest I had ever been. The hospital setting, with its clinical starkness broken only by a windowed greyness of the brutal city outside, only served to reinforce that feeling. I had never felt so alone and lost. As I read the pages of the book, I started to realise that I was indeed living a modern version of the story and came to realise Orwell's insights into poverty as my reality, and this was frightening. I truly felt physiological and physically destroyed, and having grown up in a society whose right-winged middle class seemed to feel they could judge and dictate to those whose income was lower resonated with me and made me angry. At that moment, I had become the victim of circumstance, albeit I had largely put myself there. Apart from the boredom and complications that came with abject poverty, Orwell also described the liberation that it presented. It was a poignant moment sitting in that hospital bed in London, wired up to an ECG machine, largely anaemic from the lack of blood, for it was the first time I had experienced one of three of my worst fears: poverty. However, perhaps just like the lost generation of writers, the likes of Hemingway, Fitzgerald and Orwell himself who had moved to bohemian Paris in the 1920s to observe and thus create, I somehow knew that I was more of an observer than a victim of the present circumstance. The combination of my sense of entitlement and a very strong instinct to survive, combined with my now highly developed sense of ruthlessness, would sooner rather than later deliver me out of my wretched situation. That period of living on the margins had a major impact on my life choices going forward. It was instrumental in honing my work ethic and was a major factor in not getting married and having a family. But most importantly, it helped define one of my core values, that of independence, independence from society, work and culture. I figured if I could transcend most of society's norms and expectations, the rat race, I would achieve maximum freedom, which would allow me to punch well above my weight. I wanted to be the personification of a blue water navy, operating globally without the need for a safe harbour and having total control of my environment.

The trial lasted six days, during which time, I remained in the hospital under strict supervision. On the last day after signing more forms, I was discharged and told to come back for a check-up in two weeks, after which I would be presented with a cash-cheque for my efforts. After being discharged, I didn't waste any time registering for another. In 1996, you needed to register with those individual hospitals that were running the trials. The trick was getting those numbers and having your calls answered. There was far more demand than supply when it came to willing participants, as I found out and all the hospitals ran on the same auspicious of providing a manned number for one hour a day on certain days, each hospital having its own schedule. This required spending an hour or two on the phone every day until I was accepted into another trial. I had calculated that I had only needed two trials to fulfil my funding requirements for my next trip. The second trial I was accepted too would last three weeks; however, unlike the first one, it would require three drug ingestions managed over a two-day hospital stay for a period of three consecutive weeks. On the admission form, they actually asked if you had been involved in another trial within the last six months. I chose to perpetuate a lie when answering that and many other questions related to my drug and alcohol intake of recent months. Threats of disqualification and hyperbolic warnings concerning my health that were highlighted on the forms and in the admission interviews did nothing to shake my resolve. If Danial could do it and get away with it, I was going to too. At the start of my second trial, I could almost smell success with regards to my end goal of realising my stated amount of funds that I had budgeted. I would need to travel to South America for three months. Like the first, the second trial, a third stage human trial concerning a Parkinson's drug, went without a hitch. I still kept my vanilla job at the karting place, and when I wasn't in hospital sacrificing my body for the benefit of big pharma, I would diligently be pulling cars out of tire walls, dressed in my fireproof suit, flag in hand. Sometimes I would do a red-eye after I checked out of the hospital, which, thinking back, probably wasn't the smartest decision, albeit the hospital fed me better than I ever ate myself at home, I could feel the lethargy caused by the lack of blood kicking in when doing some heavy pulling on the circuit. By this time, I had become a seasoned professional at my task of keeping that racetrack going like a Swiss clock. Not long after I had joined some of the senior race marshals had learned I had a background in computer science and thus gave me the opportunity to choreograph the races from the control room. The heart of the system was based on default configurations set up by the manufacturer. However, with a little programming knowledge, you could tweak the system with great effect. This suited me and the business. They must have saved thousands on consultancy fees, and I saved my legs. However, I was still made to do my duty on the track, which, to be honest, I enjoyed. I had the greatest respect for the guys working there; some like me were a revolving door and were using it as purely a stepping stone to supplement studies or travel agendas. Otherwise, they were men in their 30s with families, and this was their primary source of income. They tended to be much older and more on tenterhooks when it came to the whims of the two miserable owners. There was a real sense of comradery in the workplace. It was the first time I had experienced a work ethic that transcended the fact that we were just doing a job. It really felt like we were a team, and every race was treated as a mission, and like every mission, it required everybody to pull together. It didn't matter if we were on minimum wage or we would have to clean the track for free after. It was the closest I had gotten to experience almost paramilitary-style male bonding as an adult. It was a revelry I often visited in my mind during my later working life.

Seemingly, my reading list was in total synchronicity with regards to my status quo, as near the end of my time in London, I had started yet another one of George Orwell's classics, Keep the Aspidistra Flying. Much like Down and Out in Paris and London, I seemed to be living a life very similar to the protagonist Gordon Comstock, a bedraggled man living in 1930s' London on a mission to embrace his most authentic self. In doing so, he forwent life's luxuries and lived in self-imposed poverty with the sole purpose of realising his goal to become a poet, marginalising himself to the point that society had dejected him. Even the girl he so badly wanted a relationship with was kept at bay by his self-fulfilling prophecy, driven by his belief that without money, he was not worth anything, yet his sole aim was to rebel against the so-called money god. I was easily able to relate to the satire; my need to make it at all costs had left me rather devoid of any life outside that of pursuing my goal of travelling, I wore my self-imposed poverty like a badge of honour; delayed gratification became a lifestyle of epic proportions. If I could save a pound and walk ten miles, I would; if I could not buy food, I would. I had become a total financial anorexic. Much like Gordon Comstock, I had never thought about entertaining any relationships during my entire time in London for fear of exposing myself. I had become a monster in my single-minded pursuit of my goals. Thinking back, I should have been more like Gorden Gecko of Wolf of Wall Street notoriety than Gordon Comstock; I had become one of my worst fears, a man with a scarcity mindset.

My two insights with regards to the Orwellian novels were manifested in a letter to Kim, whom by now I had not heard of or spoken to since my last call; I put through to her in Newark Airport. Still, I somehow felt compelled to write to her. I had written to her briefly when I had moved into the house in Shepherds Bush, more to notify her of my address and had even tried to call her once with one of those BT phone cards, which I had splurged on one day; alas, after a few too many expensive one-sided conversations with a rather recalcitrant voicemail box, I gave up.

My last weeks in London were spent buying airline tickets and doing research on Caracas, my next destination, whilst working my notice at the karting place. The atmosphere in the house became almost hostile towards me as news of me subjecting myself to medical tests came to light. Nobody seemed to understand why I would be taking such huge risks with my health; I was judged harshly and made to feel it. My argument of course was simple. I would be given small doses or drugs made under the most precise conditions by doctors in world-class hospitals and paid handsomely in return, tax-free. They would consume drugs made in makeshift labs or, worse, shipped in, using the orifices of drug mules, with no idea of their chemical composition and pay for the privilege. I believed I had the winning argument, and at this stage, pushed as far as I could, often to comments about my supposedly malaise and anaemic look. In fact, I think it was the only time the Kiwis in the front room actually made mention of anything that came remotely close to an opinion.

Making the trip to Heathrow Airport to rendezvous with my dad as we had agreed to meet up again on his return trip was the only event of note during my last days in London.

Like the previous time, I made the arduous journey to Heathrow and waited for him in the 'Arrivals' hall. I had not expected him to want to see me again on his return trip. Our meeting lasted all of fifteen minutes, during which time he rather stoically chatted about his holiday and certain family members; just before leaving, he presented me with a gift, a shrink-wrapped Irish fish, which I presumed he had been given as a present himself. I suspected that rather than throwing it away as getting past South African Customs would have been impossible, he thought to charitably give it to his struggling son. The symbolism of the fish being transferred from the puritan to the pagan was not lost on me, and it was a fitting gesture insofar I could understand the absolute contempt my father held for me and my lifestyle choices. His aloofness put paid to any misconstrued kindness that might have been on display to those unfamiliar with him. Shortly after we shook hands, I watched him saunter off to the 'Departures' hall. It would take him another twenty years to visit me again. That evening, I struck a deal with the Polish girl that lived at the foot of my bed to share the fish. We agreed to share the fish if she prepared and cooked it; this worked out well and in an almost Biblical-like event, we shared our last supper together.

Caracas

Nothing went to plan with my travel to Caracas; the fact that I ended up spending the whole night drinking at a bar before my flight didn't help. My itinerary involved a connection via Amsterdam, and to my dismay, my flight from London was delayed just long enough for me to see my connection taxiing down the runway. After some queuing and discussions at the KLM transit desk, I soon found myself with a new itinerary in hand. Due to the fact that there was only one KLM flight a day to Caracas, I had rather unceremoniously been rerouted via NYC. Whilst waiting at the gate in Schiphol – still one of my favourite airport experiences in the world – I found my attention focussing on a pretty blonde girl milling around waiting on the same flight. I remember she held my interest for a while; I wasn't really sure why but pretty blonde girls were a dime a dozen in this airport, but for some reason, this one commanded my gaze. I quickly dismissed it as a side effect of my hangover. It felt surreal to be going back to NYC, a city I had landed in but eight months ago, at that stage the gateway to my new life, now it almost felt routine. Except for my thoughts wondering if my luggage had been as successful as I, at being rerouted, the flight went without a hitch, and I soon found myself at JFK. The ugly 1960s' brutalist form that is JFK strikes a stark contrast when compared to the chic efficient European structure that is Schiphol. It's almost a warning of sorts. The grey cement walls and threadbare carpets seem suggestive of a society that puts a low premium on the value of public services to the masses or, even worse, serves as a deterrent to people from faraway lands, and this in a city that prides itself as being a sanctuary with a blue heart. When compared to the social egalitarian paradise that is the Netherland's, with its bright modern accessible gateway of an airport, JFK is laughable. Rather frustratingly, when you make a connection in the USA, you need to clear immigration. What had struck me as novel on my first trip here, the airport and its procedures, had by now been rendered almost third-world nuance. Later that evening, whilst waiting for my backpack to appear on the baggage carousel, I found myself staring at the same pretty blonde girl that had captured my attention before the flight. At this stage, there were only the two of us, as everybody else seemed to have been lucky enough to be reunited with their luggage. On seeing her again, I approached her and asked her if NYC was her destination; to my joy, she explained she too was on her way to Caracas and like myself had missed her connection that morning coming in from Hamburg. Her name was Agatha, Polish-born, adopted and raised in Hamburg; having spent the previous summer on an exchange programme in Venezuela, she was going back to visit her host family. The synchronicity chapter from the Celestine prophecy that I had read not too far from this very airport flashed in my mind's eye as I smiled to myself. After chatting a few minutes more, we realised that our luggage would not be coming and that due to our short connection time, we would have to deal with it in Caracas.

Just as we were about to set off to the gate, she, in a minx-like manner, suggested we forget the connection and spend the evening in NYC together, as she had never been. Tempting as it was, I managed to persuade her to keep to the plan, thinking back that if I had not been there recently, I might have accepted the offer. An hour later, I found myself in a plane where the passengers all spoke Spanish going to a city I had no idea about, sitting next to a girl I had just met. It was the first time I started to realise that I may have again proverbially bitten off more than I could chew. The culture shock I experienced sitting in that plane was overwhelming, and I was grateful to have met Agatha.

Disembarking in Caracas a few hours later was a real Wizard of Oz moment. Realising I wasn't in Europe anymore was exacerbated by the heat and humidity that reached out and choked me like mustard gas, notwithstanding the brutal heat the airport was crawling with short Hispanic types sporting Fidel Castro moustaches. Arriving without my luggage didn't help my anxiety any more than Agatha did by running off to her friends and disappearing into the Castro soup that was the awaiting crowd. By this stage, I hadn't been to sleep for two nights and still had on the same clothes, with the beer stains serving as evidence that it hadn't been a nightmare but was real. I decided against my better judgment, as I truly believed it was a lost cause, to fill out a lost luggage form, which I picked up from one of the disinterested ground staff in the terminal building. Not that there was anything valuable packed, it was more the psychological aspect of the pseudo nakedness I felt which I wanted to combat; there is something rather unnatural about walking into a strange country with only the clothes on one's back, credit card and passport. Like a comfort blanket, your luggage is what gives you that added security that you have something when facing the unknown, at least it was like that for me. To my surprise, a few minutes later, Agatha returned and beckoned for me to follow her as she had organised for her ride to give another traveller, a German businessman, a lift to the Hilton Airport hotel. She explained they would drop me off there too, as getting a taxi from the airport would be like negotiating with Ali Baba and his 40 thieves at four in the morning. I reluctantly accepted under protest that unlike Hans from Hamburg, I wasn't armed with an expense account to peddle the wares of some big conglomerate based in Europe; I was but a mere backpacker with the budget for a few months and staying even one night in the Hilton would have exacted a large chunk of change, especially with the walk-in rate. She simply ignored me in a take-it or leave-it way. Like an anxious puppy, I followed her, my mind racing to see a way out of this conundrum. In the car, we were met by a German businessman, whose name I never got, and a short guy with long black hair, the driver, who seemed to remind me of Mowgli from the Jungle Book. The drive out of the airport was accompanied by soft Spanish mutterings of Agatha and the Mowgli lookalike. In an almost transmogrifying feat, Agatha slipped into her Venezuelan persona; clearly, she had not skimped on the language classes the last time she was here. She seemed to almost not have flown in with me; it almost felt like she had always been here. The road was dark and in a state of total disrepair, a three-lane highway with only a single lane operable, flanked by cheek-by-jowl shantytowns on either side, fires burning and spotlights interspersed the urban depravity in an ad hoc manner. In the distance, the airport Hilton, barricaded away, shone like a beacon of luxury in the midst of the ruinous landscape. As we pulled up to the hotel and came to a stop, Agatha turned to the businessman and muttered what seemed like a goodbye in German, and as he was getting out, she turned to me and almost commanded me that I will be also staying there that night, to which I again replied it was not an option. On hearing my panicked response, the short Venezuelan guy in the driver's seat turned to me and asked in perfect English where I had planned to stay that evening. I quickly orientated my map and showed him the area in the city that my research had flagged up as an area with budget hotels. He nervously responded that the chances of being murdered in that area were 50/50; I was stunned and fell silent. However, he soon allayed my fears by suggesting that I accompany them to Agatha's host family and then he would drive me to his area where there were more reasonable hotels on offer when compared to the Hilton. I gratuitously accepted the offer.

The route into Caracas from the airport winds its way from the ocean, graciously up the side of the valley hills that surround the city. That night, the city waited until the last moment to reveal itself; driving through the last few miles before entering the metropole gave no hint to the uninitiated visitor of what to expect. Then suddenly in an almost shock and awe scenario, it was suddenly just there, miles and miles of skyscrapers, shoehorned into a valley and bound together by freeways; the fact it was dark only added to the surreality of the moment, with the city lights given it an almost lava-like feel, a glowing molasses structure that would not have seemed out of a place in a terminator movie or similar. The drive to Agatha's host family took longer than expected; the scale of the city was immense and the juxtaposition of wealth and depravity that co-existed side by side resonated comfortably with me. This was the type of world I came from; for me, it was as normal as brushing your teeth in the morning. The only difference being that in South Africa, the depravity was better hidden for the most part. Caracas seemed to embrace the two worlds, by having each positioned with a perfect view of the other in almost twisted cohabitation acceptance. The wealth on display was also more flamboyant in an almost USA-over-the-top style. A clear manifestation of this was both the type of cars that were driven and secondly the style and scale of the monster buildings that were on show. After arriving in an upper middle-class suburb, I waited in the car whilst this Mowgli-looking guy, who by now I had come to learn was some kind of boyfriend to Agatha, said goodbye to her. By this time, it was close to 5 in the morning, and I was in desperate need of a bed. Unfortunately for me, he lived on the other side of the city in a similar yet far away upper middle-class neighbourhood. On arrival, I set about knocking on a few hotel doors to negotiate a bed for what was left of the night whilst this kind stranger I had just met a few hours earlier waited for me in his car. Most hotels were bolted down for the evening, which made me think what the situation would have been like in the area I had originally planned to stay in if this was a supposedly good area. The best response I got after a few attempts was to wave and fob me off. On returning to the car, I felt a sense of hopelessness and kindly asked if I could crash on his couch just for a few hours just to get some sleep to recuperate. Being exhausted himself, Elias, his real name, gleefully accepted, and we sped off to his parents' house.

Late next morning, I opened my eyes after sleeping for the first time in two days and found myself on top of a bunk bed in a dark room. On leaving the room a few minutes later, I was met by a beautiful Colombian woman in the kitchen doing chores. She smiled and looked at me in a type of strange fascination as I did her. After a brief interlude of nothing, she asked me something in Spanish; thankfully, at that stage, the mum of the house arrived and introduced herself in English and offered the maid to make me breakfast, which I gratefully accepted. She was a professional-looking woman whom I later learned was a practicing dentist married to an architect. The house had a heavy dark look and feel, seemingly to keep the sun's heat out, interspersed with large bulky furniture and ornaments. Whilst eating my breakfast, Elias arrived and asked me to join him for the day running a few errands if I had time; seemingly, the guy had given me his room to sleep in and taken the spare room for himself.

My original plan was to spend one day in this unforgiving city and move on quickly to a beach town before over-landing it to Columbia. The reality turned out to be very different. After that first day, Elias and I realised that we had many similarities and shared views, and we quickly became friends, and, as a result, my stay in this city went from the planned one day to over a month. Elias, a year younger than I was, was a full-time student, which served two purposes those days in Venezuela; it kept him engaged in a trajectory that might later result in a paid profession, and more importantly, it kept him out of the army. The latter resonated with me as I had to employ the same tactics to avoid the draft myself. However, the difference being that in Venezuela you could be carded at any time by any soldier or police officer, and if you were not able to prove on the spot you were entitled to an exemption, the military were fully within their rights to haul you off and press you into service. Elias sporting long hair was a standout target; add me, a pasty face gringo, to the mix, and you had a red rag to a bull situation with regards to these 18/19-year-old soldiers that manned the multitude of checkpoints that strangled the city.

With its military checkpoints, boomed off middle-class areas, high walls, heightened sense of anxiety, lack of stability, power outages and rampant corruption, Caracas was a city like no other I had ever experienced; however, it came with such a sense of familiarity that it almost felt home. It soon became apparent to me that Venezuela was a window into the future of South Africa. The country I had left almost a year ago had already started to reveal its future in small fits and starts, but in my opinion was about ten years away from contemporary Venezuela. Where populist politics, scapegoating and pseudo-Marxist doctrine plied with the sole purpose of enriching the cadres at the top of the pig trough was the order of the day. The experience of having seen into the future was an invaluable opportunity. I made sure my decisions going forward in my life capitalised on the insight as much as possible – the overarching design change to my life I adopted – that I was left without any doubt that I should steer away from my country of origin.

Surreality and Escape

Notwithstanding the glaring depravity, wealth and strong-arm tactics employed by the state to keep control, life was quite normal and if you were middle class; I would argue it was even better than the equivalent class in Western Europe those days. Elias had a side hustle supplying the local Rave scene with alcohol. Rave music was very niche and up and coming in Caracas those days and privy to the monied only. I quickly settled into a routine that involved me shadowing him on his daily activities and so became quickly immersed in all his business dealings and the like, so much so it didn't take long to feel at home in my new surroundings. Staying with him at his parents' house was welcomed and even encouraged; his parents seemed to think that I would be a positive influence on his life, and the fact we enjoyed each other's company so much, it just seemed natural to stay.

Some days, we would drive to his university, attend lectures and while away our time discussing everything and nothing with his friends and acquaintances; other days, we would be hard at work organising the logistics of the next event. Nights would be spent fraternising with socialites, friends and other expats, all somehow connected to the rave scene. The rave events would be organised in secret weeks in advance; the information and locations of these events would be spread by word-of-mouth only, often during house parties held by one or another socialite in and around the city. Within days of having arrived in the city, I found myself at the dead centre of the scene; never in my life had I been privy to such social status in any place I had lived, let alone London where I lived a hermit's life for the most part. To say I loved every minute of my newfound life would be an understatement. Most times they would be held in artists' residences or luxury penthouses on the top of 50-storey buildings, filled to the ceiling with beautiful Venezuelan women, some of the world's most beautiful I had seen in my life, and endless supply of free drugs, cocaine being the most prominent. I embraced all on offer in excess and soon became addicted to the drugs and lifestyle. My plan to overland it to Peru was put on hold indefinitely, moreover, at that stage, I paid little or no thought to returning to Europe at all. Days for me would start at about one in the afternoon, breakfast consisting of a coffee and a line of cocaine and would end at about four in the morning. After about two weeks, I had started to lose my sense of reality and entered the realm of the surreal. Once the rave events were announced, it was our job to supply the alcohol; this involved going to large liquor outlets on the outskirts of the city and ordering pallets of water, mixers and alcohol, after which they would be placed outside on the pavement for us. We would always have two security guards we would hire on hand to protect the merchandise. Once placed on the pavement, we would look for a suitable truck that we thought would have the capacity to haul everything to the remote area in question. In practise, this meant watching the road and flagging down anything that seemed capable that

144

would pass. This was actually easier than it sounds and seemed like the modus operandi in the city at that time. Once we had negotiated and paid the hauler in question his rate, we would round up a few unemployed that were dime a dozen those days and pay them a stipend to help us load the truck. Due to the illegal nature of the events, the location was on a need-to-know bases only, and most of the time, we would make sure the haulers were sufficiently bribed to keep their silence; moreover, we made sure to deliver everything on that evening just before the event kicked off to minimise the risk of discovery by the authorities. The rule was once the event started, you couldn't leave; seemingly draconian but necessary to protect everyone. It was, however, very easy enough to enforce, as keys were taken away on arrival and the remoteness of the areas that were used as locations those days, often many miles away from the city in the surrounding hills, guaranteed a pseudo lockdown. Of course, everyone coming there knew the rules and were happy to trade their keys and freedom for a night of total debauchery. Elias and I would take it in turns running the bar; others pitched in as well; it seemed less about making money than about being part of something, something freeing. Interestingly, I would run into Agatha at both the house parties and events, and after a while, it dawned on me that she had also managed to get addicted to the lifestyle on offer and thus had made the trip back.

It was a way the intellectual kids could transcend the drab of everyday dystopia without leaving the country, as I had done. Most of them didn't have the luxury of a powerful second passport like me and were hobbled by a diminishing currency, something I had recently become all too familiar with. These events were like a window onto a world that was inaccessible to them. In this world, the rules were different; there were no soldiers waiting to drag you off to fight an existential threat – no overbearing bureaucracy that served no purpose but to saddle the masses with a burdensome tax that would further exacerbate their feelings of hopelessness – of self-censorship that robbed people of free-thinking like some awful cult. There, at that moment, for one evening, people from all over the world, albeit mostly local, would stage a defiant counter-revolutionary protest against the status quo; everything was on the table, nothing was banned. It had its dark sides I don't deny, the decadence, the drugs and not everybody there had the same idealistic view and thus came as leeches to exploit. However, it was something, and it was ours. Years later, I came to realise corporate USA with its chains of eateries and coffee shops underpinned by the Hollywood propaganda machine had indeed figured out how to tap into the same energy of people's desire to escape, if but only for a few minutes or hours into something more bearable than then their humdrum lives. What better way to escape the local slum, township, barrio or suburb than to enter a Starbucks or the like and buy a shrink-wrapped off the shelf escape experience. Perfected at source and tailored to local needs and nuances. Walking into these places feeds off the need to detach and escape the brutality of life's routine. It is less about the coffee or the food on offer; it's more about offering those, without the means, to salivate, byte and savour that which is denied to them by default. I often experienced the same need for a byte-sized escape years later whilst living in the Netherlands, a rich modern social egalitarian country that has a reputation for being a sanctuary country, with its citizens wanting for nothing. Routine life in the Netherlands was for me a dull, drab, windswept experience; its people and language combining to have the social charms of a blunt instrument, and thus I found myself needing to escape the staunch Calvinist virtues that seemed to permeate Dutch life at every level. My go-to escape those days was the Hardrock in Amsterdam, a sanctuary of American consumerism and customer service with all the trappings that I so craved. The hour or so I would spend there would be like a vacation giving me much-needed energy to combat the drabness of Dutch life in all its perfectness. Although the freedom of choice and lifestyle difference between the Netherlands and the US is insignificant when compared to the situation on the ground in Caracas those days, I still found myself in dire need to escape. I could only imagine the draw such franchises would have on for example the youth in Moscow region or La Paz.

The line between reality and fantasy started to blur, and by week three, I had developed a cocaine habit that seemed to show no sign of abating. No matter how much of the stuff I took, I wanted more. I consumed it for breakfast, lunch and supper. One morning after stumbling out of bed still in a hungover state, I slipped and bashed my head on the slater veranda; with blood pouring out of my head, I just sat there whilst Elias quickly squeezed some aloe vera from a garden cactus and applied it to my head. Five minutes later, we were doing lines on the veranda, with no thought to the gash on my head, which I still sport today as a scar.

Life in Caracas didn't only revolve around cocaine and the rave scene; I often ventured out on my own during those days, getting some distance from Elias and his circle of friends. During the first few days, I spent an inordinate amount of time trying to salvage my backpack, which I hadn't seen since London. KLM had an office in town, and I was there most mornings, demanding answers and progress. The 100 USD payoff for lost luggage was not enough to fob me off; eventually, after much perseverance, I received a call to retrieve my backpack at the airport. Whilst waiting for it to pop onto the baggage carousel, I remember hearing the woman representing the airline's ground staff telling me that this never happens, referring to the fact I was successfully able to retrieve my backpack. I was not going to just accept the loss of my bag without a fight; good thing too, I still have it 20 years later. The local bar scene in the suburb I lived in was quite lively, and oftentimes, I would venture out on my own as if to entice lady serendipity. Women were only too interested in a gringo like me even if only for a few hours, but I wasn't saying no; however, on one such night, I ran into two young German guys who, like me, were on a trip to nowhere and had gotten stuck in Caracas. In some sense, they became my link to the outside world insofar as whenever I was with them, I had no access to drugs. They were also keen on exploratory trips in and around the country, and on one such occasion, I accompanied them on such a trip to the mountainous region around Merida near the great lake Maracaibo. The lake is insignificant except for the fact it hides one of the biggest oil deposits in the world and, as such, had contributed to giving Venezuela its incredible wealth those days. The trip consisted of us bussing it to the mountains and hiking the numerous trails on offer. These guys were typical of a lot of German blokes I met those days, having signed themselves up for endless years of meaningless tertiary education, in their case majoring in South East Asia studies. They spent the years of free education and interest-free study loans traveling around the world on a whim and drinking beer. One of them actually had a more substantiated reason for wasting years of taxpayers money on their frivolous education and, by implication, their international travels: avoiding the German draft. Those days, the draft still existed in some European countries, and if you were unlikely to be selected, the best way out was a subsidised meaningless education. Not that you would be anyway put in harm's way as a soldier, but it certainly prevented a wasted year or two of drinking beer in barracks in Baden blackhole somewhere. Days were spent hiking around the many trails that snaked through the beautiful landscape that proved the backdrop to Merida; nights were spent around a fire stargazing. The night sky was some of clearest on offer in the country; it wasn't for nothing the National Astronomical Observatory had set up shop here many years before. I was grateful for the change of scenery, and after a few days away from my feverous drug-filled Caracas life that had become my routine, I had hatched a plan to leave Venezuela. I realised I just couldn't continue down the same route and expect a good outcome, so for the sake of my self-preservation, I decided to resurrect my original travel itinerary, with a major amendment: I was going to forgo the overland stretch via Columbia. I had been warned countless times whilst speaking to the locals in and around Merida that it would be at great personal risk considering the perilous situation on the border with regards the FARC and other bandits exploiting the ungovernable territory. I had heard similar warnings in Caracas, and considering the non-existence of my Spanish and the fact I was a lone traveller, I decided to take the risk off the table. On my return to Caracas a few days later, I secretly bought an airline ticket to Ecuador

149

with a short layover in Costa Rica. The date of the ticket was purposely set to coincide with the day after the next organised rave event, an early morning flight, about a week away. This would allow me to fulfil my obligations to the people that were counting on me. I decided not to tell anybody in order to give me the best chance of escape. I was fighting an internal battle with addiction, not only to the drug but the lifestyle and social status. After having spent three months living in London literally fighting to keep my head above water with the social status of no more than a beggar, life in Venezuela was pure bliss. The next few days felt like I had a double life; the vanilla existence according to the seven deadly sins went as prescribed, whilst in the back of my mind, I knew I had this escape plan and was reticent to tell anyone. Apart from being slightly more melancholic than usual, I don't think anyone noticed. I awoke with a heightened sense of anxiety the day of the event. I was getting ready to say goodbye to my addictions, and the feeling of morning precipitated my every emotion. It's a strange feeling keeping a secret; I never felt comfortable doing it but knew it was necessary for my survival. I had lost control in a place as foreign as could be. Surreal was real. I would miss my friend and my life, but something, my sense of self-preservation was overwhelming. I just hoped that by evening, I would have the strength to exact my plan and not capitulate to weakness. I was only 21 but could see this as a major fork in the road, and I needed to make the right choice. I wasn't blessed with an inheritance, trust fund, connections or talent; life was going to require a sober mind and hard work to eke out an existence. The routine before the event went as prescribed, and by late afternoon, we were on our way to the secret rendezvous point that was to be the location for that night's party. In the back of my mind, I was trying to solve how I would escape from the place just before the lockdown was imposed, as once in, nobody was allowed to leave, and I couldn't see any of these organisers giving me a lift out, the risk was too great.

The event that evening's event was in a particularly remote place about 25 km outside of the city behind the slum areas in a wooded area on the edge of a long since forsaken industrial compound, a truly apocalyptic setting, a most perfect backdrop to the planned event. On arrival, I quickly set about setting up the bar and organising the alcohol for the evening; inside, my heart was racing. I needed to get it done and get out somehow without being caught; suddenly, I felt like I was in a hostile environment. All the people I had come to know so well during the last weeks suddenly seemed to be more like my captors than friends. I could imagine people trying to escape cults having the same emotions on realising how manipulated and controlled they have become. To be honest, what is the difference between cocaine or an existential spirit or a drug dealer and a guru; both peddle their drug of choice to exact control for the sole purpose of enriching themselves. By the time I had packed my last crate of alcohol, I noticed the truck that had brought up the alcohol and gotten itself parked in behind some of the first punters that had already started arriving, I, without thinking, quickly made my way down to the vicinity and climbed on the back and waited patiently for it to leave, hoping beyond hope it would take me back to the city and not somewhere else. I felt terrible for not saying goodbye, but in my mind's eye, I felt I really had no choice. After a bumpy start-stop ride, I soon found myself in the outskirts of the city and hopped off, making use of the bus and metro to go back to Elias' parents' house. On my return, I found Elias's parents at home and explained that I needed a lift to the bus airport bus stop the next morning; they kindly agreed without discussion. The rest of the evening was spent packing and mentally preparing for what lay ahead of me, which, to be honest, at that stage, was simply a flight to Ecuador with no real plan after. Penning a letter to Kim that evening also helped me to focus on the task ahead. In the letter, which would be my last to her, I explained the depths of self-destruction I had plumbed in the last few weeks, sparing little or no details of the havoc I had wrecked on my physical and mental state and how I now found myself in a state of addiction for which there was a chance I would not ever escape. Kim, at this stage, didn't represent more than a mailing address for which to write to, as it had been more than eight months since I had had any correspondence with her. Still, I had hoped I would have at least one letter waiting for me at my old address in London and clung to that.

The Andes

The next morning, I awoke early and, as promised, was given a lift to the airport bus terminus. A few hours later, I was on my way to Costa Rica to catch my connection to Quito, Ecuador. This was going to be the start of my real traveling. The previous six weeks or so had been some of the most surreal and intense times of my life, but 20 years later, as I write this book, I would without a doubt repeat it given the chance. I landed in Quito late that evening, now armed with rudimentary Spanish, which I had garnered in Venezuela, and negotiated a taxi to the old town where I had decided to lay up for a few days whilst putting some sort of plan together. The old town was a charming quarter heralding back to the old colonist days, and I thought I would feel more comfortable than in the up-and-coming chic backpacker part of town that I guessed would be overrun with annoying entitled Americans and Europeans alike. My first experience of Quito was literally shocking; on entering my shoddy hotel room, I fumbled around for the light switch and managed to connect with live electrical current and, with a bang, landed on the floor. After a few moments writhing in pain, more from landing on the floor than the electric shock, I decided to forgo the luxury of light and crawled into bed. The next morning, I could see the reason. In typical third-world improvisation, they had funnelled the radio and bed lamp wires into the plug socket, obviously cheaper than two plugs and an adapter, and I had managed to touch both. Interestingly enough, unlike South African, UK and Maltese plugs, the US and European plugs don't have on-off switches; plugs are in or out. I had always thought that was a good idea; since that day I am more sceptical. Surprisingly, it didn't take me long to put paid to the drug habit that had bedevilled me on a daily basis whilst in Caracas, and I soon started to regain my sense of reality. I was happy about this and quickly found myself easing into the backpacking role. As usual, I met loads of people whilst frequenting the local bar scene in the evenings; for the most part, I would meet entitled Europeans and American types that seemed to masquerade as lords and masters of the city. However, on my penultimate evening before leaving the city, I met an eccentric bloke from the UK, Colin, a few years older than I, in his late twenties. He caught my attention, as he was the only guy I had ever met to travel in a two-piece suit and bowler hat with a briefcase. His story was equally unique. He had come to that part of the world to seek work as a water engineer, capitalising on the then devastating effect El-Niño – the warming of the ocean surface or above-average sea surface temperatures in the central and eastern tropical Pacific Ocean – which was having a devastating effect on the pacific countries in South America, causing flooding, destruction and general havoc. After a few drinks and an interesting chat, we decided to team up and do the next leg of our journey together. Due to the devastation to the Pacific highway caused by EL-Niño at the time, we had no choice but to bus it through the mountains on our way to the Peruvian border. Two days later, we met as planned at the international bus station and boarded a bus bound for Cuenca, a nondescript town serving as a waypoint on our way south. The roads were a mix of mud and mush, and the journey took far longer than expected. Colin, who was a dab hand at Spanish, took it upon himself to give me a more formalised introduction into the basics of the language; as I had nothing else to do sitting on that bus, I gratefully accepted. The travelling was hard and oftentimes, we would have to get out and either help to push the bus or retrieve our belongings and walk to lighten the load for a km or two. On reaching Cuenca, we jumped in a taxi to the hotel area. The driver and Colin quickly got into a discussion in Spanish, whilst I stared out the window at the slum of a town we had arrived in. The weather being overcast only exacerbated the awfulness of the townscape, reminding me a little of Tower Hamlets in London. Suddenly, Colin turned to me and let me in on the discussion that had ensued between him and the driver since getting into the taxi. Seemingly, the driver emanated from Cuba, had a fat Russian wife who cooked and ran after him in a truly oriental type of relationship, and, interestingly enough, suffered a limp, due to being on the receiving end of a bullet from a South African assault rifle during the border war. My initial reaction to Colin was along the lines of regret that the bullet didn't lodge in his brain. My emotional reaction surprised both of us. I had long since been a proponent against the regime I had grown up in with its offensive wars and counter-insurgency operations that reigned supreme during the late-'80s and beyond. Notwithstanding the anxiety the egregious violence that prevailed on our borders those days caused me, sometimes, to tears as I bore witness to the casualties of the day being highlighted on the eight o'clock news, akin to the closing credits on display after a movie, except that the movie was real and the actors were one-hit wonders, as were they now too dead to be cast again. Somehow, it tapped into a primaeval sense of self-preservation and almost patriotism, something I had never experienced before. Of course, even at that stage, I had enough self-awareness to realise the system had conditioned me to some extent, and there was no getting away from this; however, I felt this tapped into something deeper, a sense of wanting to protect myself and family from these Russian backed aggressors. A cacophony of events had transpired to etch this into my soul over years, a notable example being my mother teaching me to drive at the age of 12 in case we ever got involved in any roadside violence or similar that was so prevalent those days in order to able to get us out the situation. I truly believe there is part of me that if ever having been put in a difficult situation, I would not only have killed these people but enjoyed it. We only spent the night there in some run-down cheap hotel, before again boarding a bus south this time to Loja. At the bus stop, we ran into a tall American dude from NYC, Brian, who had the biggest straw hat I had seen in a while, about my age doing some traveling whilst waiting for his first semester at Brown University to start. The three of us seemed to get on very well, and he soon joined the two of us on our travels to Peru. For the next week or so, the three of us were inseparable, travelling in the most carefree and laser-fair way we could. We managed to keep each other entertained and in stitches for all jokes that we shared. The physical appearance of the three captivated many onlookers, both local and foreign. Colin, in his two-piece suit complete with a briefcase, was more suited for a day in the city of London than a ramshackle bus in the Andean mountains. Brain was over two metres, sporting surf Bermuda shorts and his umbrella sized straw hat, and me, well, being me. Brain and I bade farewell to Colin in Trujillo, Peru, where he seemed to think he would be able to secure employment, whilst we carried on to Lima together, where we shared a room in a lodgement in the middle of the city on the 30th floor of a flat building. By now, I was well out of the drug funk that I had become embroiled in, in Caracas, and albeit life was harder and not nearly as glamorous, I was grateful to be out and for the authenticity of the travel I was experiencing.

Lima, like Caracas, was a monster of a city with a few glitzy suburbs surrounded by slums. This was Brian's last stop before going back to NYC, and whilst we shared a room for those few days in Lima, we spent precious little time together. I preferred to explore my own agenda of seeking out what the nightlife had on offer, chasing women and sleeping late; other times, I would hang in the many of the city plazas and people watching. Mostly, I met groups of girls that were intrigued by foreigners, and this sometimes led to all-night benders and sometimes nothing. Lima in itself didn't interest me much. I just used it to regroup after about two weeks of hard travel. One evening on entering a random bar, I got chatting to a waitress; she seemed to take a liking to me, and I responded in my response, albeit I was very guarded and kept my distance and my mind sober. I was acuity aware I was opportunistic fodder for those with no scruples and one step from being a victim. By this stage in my life, I had such a strong conviction of who I was and wasn't and prided myself in my ability to withstand most forms of manipulation; this sometimes led to situations where I would come across as blatantly blunt and belligerent. My first experience with this had been several years before whilst attending an evangelical church retreat when I was still at high school. I had only agreed to go, as I fancied one of the girls at the church, but I was open to everything those days. The group I had joined for the event ranged from the serious diehards to the purportedly serious due to parental pressure. The town I grew up in was a typical backward right ring farm town on the edge of Cape Town, where the predominant religion was hypocritism and bigotry, fertile catchment areas for these evangelical churches. The weekend retreat took place in a campsite in a rural setting a few km outside of town and followed the normal protocol of singalong and Bible study classes, all orchestrated by the seniors of the church. I honestly tried my best to understand and participated wholeheartedly. The piste de resistance came at the last evening where everybody joined in what looked like the equivalent of the nursery rhyme enactment of 'Ring a Ring o' Roses', except instead of holding hands and swinging in and out, they were holding their hands in unison up to the ceiling as if trying to conduct lightning. The group's movement carefully manipulated by the pastor and interspersed with music and guilt soundbites moved fervently until the point where the tongues of fire would be unleashed on all those who had converted. Within minutes, there were kids falling down all around me, retching on the floor, as if struck down by a violent force, except for me of course. I am not sure how many people actually experienced the real McCoy that evening or simply played into the herd mentality, but I simply wouldn't comply no matter how much of a guilt trip was going to be brought down on me. Needless to say, afterward, I was treated with the same disdain the kids in the book *The King With no Clothes* were when they pointed out that indeed the king's new garments were nothing but a manipulative ploy. With the same contempt I had felt for that and similar situations, I snubbed the waitress at the dive bar and let her ply her trade on the next unsuspecting victim whilst I went to bed. The real drawcard in Peru was of course Machu Picchu. After taking council with a number of other travellers and locals alike, I was persuaded to invest the money in a return flight to Cusco, as the left-wing terrorist group 'The Shining Path' after being dormant for years had recently become active again. It was a well-known fact that their bandit activities of kidnapping and the like were prevalent in the overland route to Cusco. Less than a week after arriving in Lima, I wished my friend Brian goodbye and made my way to the airport for what was going to be the last leg of my South American adventure. Later that day, I found myself on an AeroPeru 727 facing backward taxiing down the runway. As a kid, I had often heard my parents speak of their initial flight experiences in these old airlines with the strange seat arrangements, more suited to a train than a plane. As uncomfortable as it was, I revelled in the novelty factor. I spent a day in Cusco mainly organising my train to the small town of Agua Caliente, which lies at the foot of the mountain on which the ancient Inca city is built. I made the conscious decision not to hike the Inca trail, as I found the prospect of walking in unison with hundreds of tourists in a supposedly serene area stomach-churning. My plan was simple: train it the day before, rent a dive for the night, get up before the sun, ramble up the mountain as fast as possible and catch the city at sunrise. As planned, early next morning, as I was navigating my way through a labyrinth of tourist buses with their sleeping drivers dotted all over the place like some makeshift refugee camp, I accidentally startled a dog who seemed to belong to one of the slumbering drivers. In an instant of pure terror, the beast had managed to sink his teeth into my ankle deep enough to draw blood. At the same time, the startled owner commanded him back whilst I broke into a pure hyperbolic rage. After I had calmed down, I thought about the implications of not having taken a tetanus shot before I left and the chances of getting rabies. With my destination so close, I decided against my better judgment to leave it up to fate and proceeded with my ramble up the mountain that morning. Thankfully, it paid off; to this day, I have yet to foam at the mouth. Moreover, I rather stupidly never sought medical help subsequently. To say the sight of the sun rising over the lost city was spectacular would be an understatement. I only spent a few hours there, and by the time the first tourist buses started arriving with their complement of fat Americans, I had already left.

Full Circle

The last two weeks before I caught my flight back to London, took me to La Paz, the capital of Bolivia. Like some of the eastern European Countries I had been to, I was really grateful not to have been born there. Poor beyond belief, La Paz is further handicapped by its altitude. Set in a valley, which, to me on face value from my days in the scouts, seemed the most unfortunate place to build a city. As scouts, we were always taught to set up camp on high ground to avoid flooding. La Paz was memorable to me, as it was the second place I managed to electrocute myself on the trip; this time, the event took place in the shower of my 1-star hotel room. The amenity of hot water had become a luxury since I had left Venezuela. The shower at my disposal had as a feature a hot water element attached to the showerhead which seemed a most useless design. However, being desperate for even lukewarm water, I fiddled to get the contraption to work. At some point, it connected via me and I was again sent hurtling to the floor with a violent bang. As I lay exposed on the cold concrete floor rather comically wrapped in the cheap plastic shower curtain, I remember having the last 12 or so months of travel flash in my mind in reverse, and for a fleeting moment, I reminisced about my life in Johannesburg. I was done and I had had enough. Not that I didn't enjoy La Paz, as by now my Spanish had become fairly decent, I was psychologically burned out. Making the trip back to Lima where my return flight would take me back to London became an arduous cacophony of third-world bus trips, dive shelters and annoying backpackers.

My South American experience was key in righting my trajectory from being overly left wing and having kept me rather centred, the call to the left I know all too well can be seductive and intoxicating to the point of being blinding. Having championed many causes, I started to realise that it was less about the cause and more about the adrenaline rush that I would get.

The relief of putting South America behind me was soon replaced with anxiety as the plane back to London took off from Lima. There was nothing and nobody waiting for me in London. I would yet again have to start from scratch, and this time, I was armed with little or no enthusiasm, and the novelty factor of traveling had been replaced with dread and anxiety. Strangely enough, all around me were parents of newly adopted babies flying back to different parts of Europe. I could never understand the appeal of children never mind taking over the responsibilities of another's offspring. I couldn't help but wonder just how different the lives of these kids were going to turn out based on this. Then I thought of Agatha herself, an adoptee from Poland that had ended up in Hamburg brought up by German parents and how we had shared the same addiction to cocaine, and in actual fact, that had been her major reason for her return to the continent, a proud day for her parents I am sure.

Landing in London the next morning was a sobering experience; the place seemed a world away from the chaos of the last few months. London and I have always had a strange relationship; as a city, it's as familiar as any I had grown up in. I have never experienced anything close to culture shock, yet it never manages to conjure any contentment in me. To this day, I never understood why. Sadly enough, I ended up back in one of those non-descript youth hostels in and around Earls Court and felt myself entering a pseudo depression. The winter weather that defines the place most of the year exacerbated the situation no end. At a loss and after visiting my previous address in a vain attempt to see if there were any letters for me from Kim, which there weren't, I decided to give a friend of mine in Dublin a call. He was actually the son of one of my father's best childhood friends, who I had met on a few trips prior to the country. Gary, an enigmatic, charming bloke, who seemed as lost as I when we met a few years before, was happy to hear from me and invited me over for his sister's 21st birthday party the following weekend. I didn't need much more persuasion than that and immediately bought my bus ticket.

There is something about English cities that makes me lose the will to live; their brutalist acid-rain-eaten grey façades cut stark apocalyptic black figures into the overcast skyscape that is England. Birmingham, seemingly the hub for those unfortunate enough to have to take the National Express bus as a means of travel, is no exception; in fact, it probably should be crowned the ugliest and twinned with somewhere in Russia, another country sporting beautiful cityscapes.

The ferry from Wales, the home of all things sheep, to Dublin is a welcome respite from the British mainland, as it gives the feeling of hope for something better. Dublin, by no means a beautiful city itself and in many ways very poor those days, seemed to have the same charm that existed in many of the Eastern European cities that I had visited during the summer. It was that charm and village-like closeness that made being there such a great experience. I was no stranger to the place and had been there several times whilst studying. In fact, the seeds of my then contemporary self had been sown all but five years before whilst on a four-week trip there, my first out of South Africa. It was there that I had started to ask the poignant questions that had led me on this adventure around the world, and it almost seemed fitting that I was back. Little did I know at that stage just how well it would work out for me. Arriving at Gary's house was always met with the warmest of welcomes, and it was one of those few places in the world where I felt totally at ease with myself those days. I found a comfortable place on Gary's bedroom floor where I bedded down for the duration of my stay. His younger sister, Lynn, whose birthday it was the coming weekend, was a classic beauty, and I secretly had a crush on her; notwithstanding her beauty, she had the outgoing personality and charm to complement her good looks. The house reminded me of a train station, people coming and going all the time and full of life, totally different from my own stoic house back in Cape Town. The birthday party came and went and I continued to stay, not having any real interest in moving back to London. Days turned into weeks until one day, at the local pub, it was suggested that I try and secure a corporate job, as the country was experiencing something of an economic renaissance. Those days, Ireland offered a young well-educated English-speaking workforce at a fraction of the cost of comparable workers on the continent, and thus it became the focus of massive offshoring enactments on the part of big US tech companies. For me, it started as a joke, perusing through the already drink-stained thumbed Irish times lying around the pub that afternoon; however, the more I thought about it, the more I liked the idea. At that stage, I was done with menial work for minimum wage and after all, I had years of computer science education behind me.

My first interview was a disaster, a tech support role for one of the large American beige box suppliers that had set up a cheap labour force those days. The job demanded basic operating system skills, which I doubt I had at that stage; however, it was my total honesty in the interview that cost me the opportunity, as when asked what team player I would make, I responded with an answer that I worked better alone. The interview reminded me of a similar experience I had when soliciting for work placement roles whilst studying. I was once requested to attend an interview for a role at one of the South African government agencies. The interview was split in two: the first part consisted of ad hoc questions in English, and the second part was to be conducted in Afrikaans, a language I detest to this day, on request that I start responding in my then second language, Afrikaans. I politely refused and explained that in solidarity with the oppressed masses, I, in principle, refused to speak the language of the oppressor. As expected, the interview came to an abrupt halt. Notwithstanding my initial interview failure in Dublin, I was eventually able to secure a software engineering job for one of the big Scandinavian telecoms companies with R&D offices in Dublin; in hindsight, a great opportunity that set me up for life.

It was during those weeks whilst hunting for work that I hatched a plan with Gary and some of his friends to recreate a mini version of my US road trip tailored for Ireland, a country I had seen precious little of outside of Dublin. The idea was simple: hire the cheapest car we could afford, pile into it and drive from town to town and figure it out as we went along. Budgets were tight, and the only car we could afford was a two-door fiat; it was going to be a tight fit for five guys, one or two being larger than average. There were only two drivers, myself and one other bloke. From Dublin, we went south to Cork and then further to Kerry. Ireland, to me, seemed to be stuck in a homogeneous time warp; outside of Dublin, it seemed everybody was Irish. In Cork, we slummed it with friends of friends in a student digs whilst participating in the national pastime of excessive drinking, followed by the indigestion of large amounts of fried chips. I have no recollection of Kerry mainly due to the alcohol abuse brought to bear on my body in Cork, but I am told it is worth a visit nonetheless.

The country lacked the core ingredient for a successful road trip; it lacked expansiveness. In South Africa and the USA, you have the luxury of vast tracts of land cut in two by miles of straight asphalt, with nothing but you and the horizon. That feeling of freedom and insignificance facilitating that introspection is what only a true road trip can give. There was none of this in Ireland; roads were mostly short, twisting and required full concentration. The country is beautiful but somehow hemmed in by thousands of years of traditional animal husbandry whilst fastidiously presided over by the watchful eye of the Catholic Church, awful. From Kerry, we drove northwest via Ennis, where I bore witness to a drunken mob almost overrun a local hamburger joint after a night out; it was like something out of the Simpsons. It was on this trip that I realised that my Irish pedigree stopped with my passport. I really felt no kinship with the overbearing egregious personality that seemed so prevalent everywhere I went. My stoicism and phlegmatism seemed better placed for the southeast of England. Don't get me wrong, I loved the people and their country, the home to so many intellectual writers and poets. I just felt like an alien; moreover, I couldn't see my father in this place at all. His aloof and pontificating ways seemed out of sync with a country whose combined personality thrived on being larger than life so to speak.

It was during that trip that one night after some heavy drinking that things took a strange turn. We had, as usual, arrived at a friend's place; this time, instead of a student digs, it was a beautiful house set in the countryside. We had arrived and, after a few brief introductions, had immediately started the night prescribed binge drinking. After a few hours of marathon alcohol abuse and as people were crawling into their respective corners to sleep, I decided to sneak into one for the rooms clearly used as an office and use the phone without permission. Feeling particularly brave, I justified the theft akin to a form of wealth distribution. In hindsight, it made no sense and was pure theft, but at the time it seemed okay. I rather nervously fiddled through my black book for a few numbers of people I hadn't contacted in months or longer. The first name that raced through my mind was Kim, the girl I had met briefly on my weekend trip to Boston. I had written to her periodically throughout the year but had never received a reply, which made sense as I had never stayed long enough to really have a return address, albeit I had made the effort on my return to London to go back to the house I had camped in for three months to check if by chance she had replied. Rather disappointingly, there had been no letter waiting for me. I nervously hid behind the desk, dialling her number rather hastily, getting the international dialling code wrong the first time. Then suddenly, I heard the sound of the other phone ringing. After a few seconds, her mother answered. After a short discussion, I hung up and dragged myself to bed on the couch.

The next day, I awoke early and took Gary aside and explained that I needed to get to Boston ASAP. We packed the car and sped back to Dublin. On arrival, I set about organising funds and buying an air ticket to Boston. I had to borrow most of the money from friends and credit-card the rest. I tried to ignore my impending job start in seven days. The next day, while in transit in Heathrow, I put another short call through to Kim, explaining that I would be in Boston in seven hours and couldn't wait to see her. She reacted with complete calmness like I was taking the local bus from a neighbouring suburb. I loved her American naivety, I embraced it. I couldn't wait to see her!

Walking up to her house that evening in Southie, which I had to find from memory, I found the door ajar. With trepidation, I knocked, waited and knocked again. "Hello," she exclaimed! When she finally appeared. "You cut your hair?" she exclaimed again.

"Hello, Kim," I replied as I embraced her in the little corridor leading into her house. It was obvious much time had passed since we had last seen each other. She seemed different, both physically and in her demeanour. She shut the front door and led me upstairs to her loft.

On the phone, her mum had briefly mentioned that Kim had been in a psychiatric hospital at the time; more details than that I had not received on the call. I was very curious about the nature of the situation that had necessitated such an extreme action. At that stage in my life, the closest I had come to meeting such people was through the book One Flew Over the Cuckoo's Nest. Not long after I had entered her loft, it became apparent that I was dealing with somebody in a rather precarious state of mind. The few details I did get from my rather subtly placed questions did nothing to satisfy my curiosity. I was instead presented with a cacophony of strange behaviour and stories that made no sense. Kim had become an actor in a self-scripted movie that seemed to be born out of her fascination with the then contemporary Play RENT, by Johanan Larson, and the artist formerly known as Prince.

She sat and explained how it was in her destiny to follow Prince and devote her life to him as his concubine of sorts. She then proceeded to play sound bytes from his various albums on her vinyl player, still a mainstay those days, which, she seemed convinced, were secret messages for her alone from the artist himself. What shocked me was her pinpoint precision in dropping the vinyl needle on the exact part of the record that she deemed to be of salient nature to her alone. I figured she would have spent days studying each and every album in detail. This was repeated with a copy of the RENT soundtrack, albeit the messages were less clear and seemingly more generic.

The next days were some of the most surreal and insightful I would ever experience in my life. The more I tried to reason with her, the more she seemed to suck me into her narrative. Hours were spent in her loft discussing the finer points of her life plan, each subsequently backed up with various passages and lyrics. Kim's mother, for her part, seemed as lost as her daughter. She would potter around the house as if in another world. I didn't have the life experience at that point in my life to see the precarious situation for what it was and felt myself becoming more and more sucked in. I realise now probably due to the amount of vested energy I had spent writing to her over the last year. Every letter I had written had in some sense captured a newly understood insight and I would share with her and only her.

A few days before my flight back to Dublin, for which I needed to take as I had a life to start, I started to feel reluctant to go back and started to look for excuses to stay. This was a guise to mask the truth of the matter, which was that I was totally intoxicated and infatuated with the situation. I felt like I was in a spider's web. I too had spent the last year escaping reality. I understood too well the appeal this mindset had. I had done it through travel; Kim had done it through imagination and prescription drugs. It seemed we had been on the same journey this year, and now we were both in a death spiral. It cannot overemphasise just how seductive the situation had become for me.

Then on the penultimate day before my flight, she presented me with all the letters I had written to her during my trip. She dumped them in front of me in a most nonchalant way. In front of me were all the letters; sadly enough, not all had been opened. This would explain why I had probably received no replies during the year. I had rationalised it to not having stayed in the same place long enough, but in reality, it was simply lack of interest. As I fumbled through the letters, I found a few diary entries she had written. Seemingly, they had been stored in the same draw as my letters, and in her haste to return the letters, she had forgotten to sort them out. Feeling rather hurt at seeing some of my letters unread, I proceeded to skim-read the entries.

What I found was shocking; seemingly, she had, on more than one occasion, befriended homeless people and taken them home. It wasn't her promiscuity that affected me; it was the fact that she had classified me as one of these types to begin with. This hit me like a ton of bricks. I realised that in effect, I had not been that different to these people when I had met her. At that point, my life flashed past me, and for once, the discipline that I had been instilled in me from my strict parents, the church and even the drill sergeant on the cadet field back in high school came to play. For the first time since I had left South Africa, I could see that I had been staring down an abyss of chaos and self-destruction for the longest time. It had been a necessary journey, but it was time for it to end. It was time to say goodbye to Kim, the personification of my alter ego and move on.

Two days later, I took my plane back to Dublin and started my new life in the corporate world, armed with the knowledge and insights that I had learned in my year of self-discovery.

It had been a poignant year; on face value, I was the same person. To the naked eye nothing had changed, yet I had somehow flipped myself around. Constitutionally, I was an entirely different person; moreover, the fact the journey had taken place in the year of '96 was not lost on me, a number which when flipped is still itself.

Daniel, for his part, never came to the same realisation and he continued to plumb the depths of chaos and self-destruction for many years until he finally hanged himself in a small town in Patagonia, Argentina. He could no longer escape the pain.

I dedicate this book to him.